Bulimic to Believer

Using Biblical Principles to Understand

Bulimia is More Than an

Eating disorder

Jamella Stroud

Bulimic to Believer: Using Biblical Principles to Understand Why Bulimia is More Than an Eating Disorder.

Copyright © 2016 by Jamella Stroud. All rights reserved.

All rights reserved. No part of this publication may be reproduce, stored in a retrieval system or transmitted in any way by means, electronic, mechanical, photocopy, recording or otherwise without the prior written permission of the author except as provided by USA copyright law.

Cover image designed copyright © Pbimbola (Fiverr) All rights reserved.

Author photo copyright © 2016 by DeAngelo Croom All rights reserved.

Edited by Monique Nixon Jus Write 4 You & Tamika L. Sims Ink Pen Diva

Scripture taken from AMPLIFIED BIBLE, AMP Copyright ® 1954, 1958, 1962, 1964, 1965, 1987 by The Lockman Foundation. All rights reserved. Used by permission. (www.Lockman .org)

Scripture quotations marked " KJV" are taken from the Holy Bible, King James Version, Holman KJV Study Bible Copyright 2012 by Holman Bible Publishers, Nashville, Tennessee. All Rights Reserved.

Scripture quotation marked "NLT" are taken from the Holy Bible, New Living Translation, Copyright 1996. Used by permission of Tyndale House Publishers, Inc. All rights reserved.

Scripture quotation marked "NKJV" are taken from The New King James Version, Thomas Nelson Publishers, Nashville: Thomas Nelson Publishers. Copyright 1982. Used by permission. All rights reserved.

This book is a memoir that provides accurate and authoritative information with regards to the subject matter covered. This information is a result of years of Bible study, research, life experience and application. They are intended as a guideline for healthy living and are not a replacement for professional counseling or medical advice. Jamella Stroud makes no warranties, representation, or guarantee regarding any particular results or outcome. Any and all express or implied warranties are disclaimed. Since the details of your situation are fact dependent, you should seek the services of a competent professional.

Published in the United States of America ISBN: 978-069273169

1. Spirituality
2. Memoir
3. Self Help

"Then they cried out to the LORD in their trouble; He saved them out of their distresses. He sent His word and healed them, and delivered them from their destructions." Psalms 107:19-20

The story of deliverance revealed by Jamella is truly amazing. She traces the acts of God as He moves her towards the healing and the freedom He has always wanted for her. You will be able to relate as she hears God's voice, but doesn't really understand the depth of the message He has for her. The impact of her deliverance from the deep heart issues must have had an amazing impact on those around her. If you are feeling down or discouraged with the challenges of life maybe like her, you should stop and listen to your heart. Could it be that the circumstances of our life are simply a reflection of our hearts? This book is more than just ordinary reading. It is a journey into the heart, a journey that ends in a blessing.

Pastor Brian Danese- treasurer, Gulf State Conference of Seventh-day Adventist

It is my desire to raise awareness about Bulimia Nervosa. It's not just a White woman's disorder, nor a skinny woman's disorder, but it was my disorder. I carried it in my heart, mind, soul and spirit for five years and it showed in every aspect of my life.

Table of Contents

Foreword vii

Facts about Bulimia Nervosa xiii

Introduction xix

Acknowledgment xxiii

Chapter 1: Bulimia A Different Perspective 1

Chapter 2: Heart of The Matter 9

Chapter 3: Food Addict 24

Chapter 4: Emotional Roller Coaster 39

Chapter 5: Financial/Business Bulimia 53

Chapter 6: You Spot It, You Got It. 97

Chapter 7: Resilient Soul 124

Chapter 8: Purpose, Passion & Perspective 152

Enrollment Offer 165

References 167

Foreword by Aprille Franks-Hunt

Pain. Purge. Purpose.

I'm not even sure where to begin here. When Jamella initially asked to me write the foreword to this masterpiece of a book – I simply agreed because she asked and is a part of my online community. We'd even met in person at an event in Birmingham, AL several months ago.

There's a reason I am sharing this, so stay with me...

As I think about it, I'm not sure I recalled the name or topic of this book after I'd agreed to her request – as I get a request several times per month, most I have to decline. After several weeks passed, a package arrived at my downtown office where it sat for a little over a week or so as I was traveling for business. Upon my return, I grabbed the package and headed to my other office where I opened it and it was in that moment I recalled the topic, Bulimia. As I read the cover letter, I thought to myself "why did she ask me to write the foreword". That said, I still didn't connect with the topic of bulimia initially until I remembered that I too, had experienced bulimia as a way of coping during a period as a teenager. For a few moments it paralyzed me because I had suppressed those behaviors so deep – and until just a couple of weeks ago I'd never admitted that I would binge on food – then throw up publicly to anyone. So while Jamella is sharing her experience from *Bulimia to Believer*, this has opened up another layer of truth and transparency for me – and hopefully it will do the same for you as you digest her truth in these pages and see a resemblance of yourself.

Now, I want to be clear, I am no bulimia expert, please defer to Jamella and other professionals for that. But what I want to share with you before you dive into this book is how we're connected through pain, purging and purpose – and how pain shows up in our lives.

Let me share a quick story with you…

My father was sergeant in the Army and children of soldiers in the Army are affectionately called Army Brats – that was me. I remember my dad being assigned to a base in Fort Campbell Kentucky when I was in the 10th grade – I attended Northeast High School in Clarksville, TN. This place was where I felt the most lost and was the onset of internal unrest in my spirit as a young woman. There had been many unforgettable life nightmares as my young mind would refer to them. At this point I was 15 years young, an over comer of sexual assault, still experiencing residual abandonment issues from being adopted, trust issues from watching the men in my life abuse the women in theirs, both verbally and physically and just being a teenager earning to navigate life. Not to mention the instability yet stable life of being in an active military family, relocating every two-three years with my parents.

I was lost, didn't know who I was – if I was coming or going and my father was also sent to the Desert Storm war in XXXXX.

This period was such a period of me really trying to "find myself" and kind of "figuring myself out" with not much help from my mother. I believe she was dealing with her own womanly stuff….and basically being a married single mom with a husband at war and away. So I kept it all in. I was binging on trauma and it showed up as food. Taking it all in, and keeping it there, until I went into the bathroom to stick my finger in my throat to remove it again. Wow, I can remember doing it and my mother asking me, "did you throw up on purpose…?"

I found that binging comes in all forms. When we are in pain, overwhelmed or confused, a release is needed and the ways we are provoked to do so are very individualistic. Because of this, I choose never to judge people for why they do certain things, as I see it, pain shows up as purging episodes differently for us all. For me, oddly the pain of being molested, afraid for my mother and my grandmother, and for myself from men showed up as me being a bully, hanging with the wrong crowd and then having multiple meaningless sexual encounters with teenage boys. At that age I didn't even like boys (men) but I truly enjoyed manipulating them to do what I allowed them to do to me. It was what I felt I could control, they were never actually controlling any part of me – it was all what I allowed and had planned. In my experience this is what Bulimia is. The way to control the one thing you can – to control one's pain through binging (consumption) and the quasi release of that pain through purging (throwing it up).

I remember understanding what I was doing – and part of it was the biggest scream for help that one can fathom. I didn't have the words at 15 years old to express what I needed or wanted. Hell, I'm not sure I even knew. I just knew that I was in pain, and lonely. After a year what I knew was I no longer wanted to hurt myself that way – and chose more sex instead of food as my binge of choice. It wasn't until my early thirty's that I began to seek ways to eliminate unhealthy binging habits.

Binging doesn't only show up in food as you can see, but in our behaviors, in what we do. For instance, the workout gym addict, the casual drug user with a successful career, the uninhibited sex with strangers, taking on grand projects, retail therapy, and gambling –

all ways of over consuming to get rid of something, an attempt to deal with something without actually dealing with the thing that needs to be dealt with. That "something" is different for us all. What has (or does) "something" represent for you? Be honest, open up – with yourself. Beloved, as you digest this book and the lessons in it, I am challenging you to think in the highest level that your mind can allow. Be open to it, be judgeless of it and you, as you discover you own freedom path to believing what is possible for you no matter what your bulimia looks like.

This book is a revelation into the one woman's pain, her purging and her now purpose and freedom to help you open up and heal.

I believe this book is the gateway to healing and will save someone's life, and I hope that the life it saves is yours.

Aprille Franks-Hunt

Facts about Bulimia Nervosa

Bulimia Nervosa is an emotional disorder involving distortion of body image and an obsessive desire to lose weight, in which bouts of extreme overeating are followed by depression and self-induced vomiting, purging or fasting; an eating disorder in which a large quantity of food is consumed in a short period of time, often followed by feelings of shame, guilt, and rejection.

Bulimia Nervosa affects 1-2% of adolescent and young adult women. Approximately 80% of bulimic patients are female. People struggling with bulimia usually appear to be of average body weight. Many bulimics recognize their behavior is unusual and perhaps dangerous to their overall health. Bulimia Nervosa is frequently associated with symptoms of depression and changes in social adjustment. Risk of death from suicide or medical complications is highly increased for eating disorders.

When someone struggles with bulimia, life is a constant battle between the desires to lose weight or stay thin and the overwhelming compulsion to binge eat.

Binging brings on guilt and shame. During an average binge, a person may consume from 3,000 to 5,000 calories in one short hour. After it ends, panic sets in and drastic measures are taken to "undo" the binge, such as taking Ex-Lax, inducing vomiting, or going for a 10-mile run. The binging and purging behavior gives the person a false feeling of control.

It's important to note that bulimia doesn't necessarily involve purging or physically eliminating the food from the body by throwing up or using laxatives, enemas, or diuretics. The bulimic often makes up for binging by fasting, exercising excessively, or going on crash diets. This also qualifies as bulimia. The chance for recovery increases, the earlier this eating disorder is detected. Therefore, it is important to be aware of some of the warning signs of Bulimia Nervosa.

Warning Signs of Bulimia Nervosa

The evidence of binge eating includes the disappearance of large amounts of food in short periods of time, or finding "wrappers" and containers indicating the consumption of large amounts of food. It also includes frequent trips to the bathroom after meals, signs and/or smells of vomiting, laxatives, or diuretics, excessive, rigid exercise regimen--despite weather, fatigue, illness, or injury, the compulsive need to "burn off" calories taken in, unusual swelling of the cheeks or jaw area; calluses on the back of the hands and knuckles from self-induced vomiting, discoloration or staining of the teeth, and the creation of lifestyle schedules or rituals to make time for binge-and-purge sessions. This includes the withdrawal from usual friends and activities. In general, behaviors and attitudes indicating that weight loss, dieting, and control of food are becoming primary concerns which continues despite injury, fatigue, or illness

Health Consequences of Bulimia Nervosa

Bulimia nervosa is extremely harmful to the body. The recurrent binge-and-purge cycles can damage the entire digestive system. Purging behaviors can lead to electrolyte and chemical imbalances in the body that affect the heart and other major organ functions. Some of the health consequences of Bulimia Nervosa include: Electrolyte imbalances that can lead to irregular heartbeats and possibly heart failure and death. Electrolyte imbalance is caused by dehydration, loss of potassium and sodium from the body as a result of purging behaviors. Inflammation and possible rupture of the esophagus from frequent vomiting tooth decay and staining from stomach acids released during frequent vomiting, chronic irregular bowel movements, and constipation as a result of laxative abuse. Gastric rupture is an uncommon, but possible side effect of binge eating.

Race, Ethnicity, and Culture

Eating disorders have historically been associated with young, White women of privilege. This is a myth. Eating disorders do not discriminate. While more research is needed in this area, we do know that the prevalence of eating disorders is similar among Non-Hispanic Whites, Hispanics, African-Americans, and Asians in the United States. Anorexia nervosa is more common among Non-Hispanic Whites.

http://www.nationaleatingdisorders.org/eating-disorders-women-color-explanations-and- implications.

There is this myth that African-American women do not suffer with eating disorders and bulimia in particular, but the women who suffer, often suffer in silence because Bulimia Nervosa is a taboo subject within the African-American community.

We have learned what Bulimia Nervosa is from the medical and research perspective. However, I would like to take bulimia a bit deeper by looking at how it sticks it toxic insidious head in other areas of life.

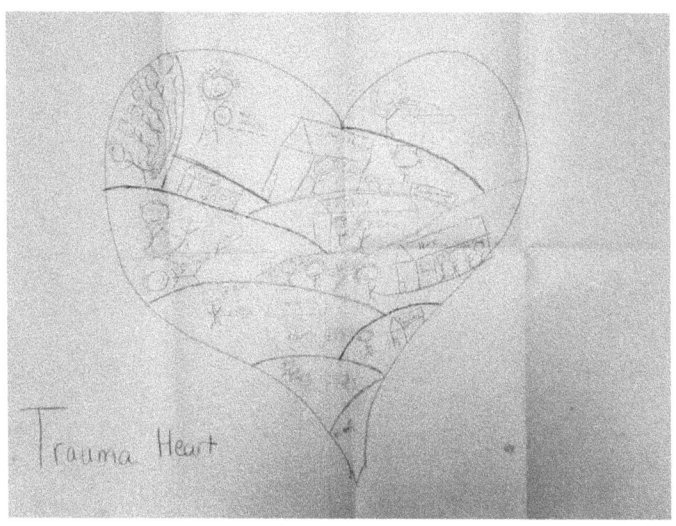

I've heard a picture is worth a thousand words; I'd like to suggest this picture is worth over 30,000 words and this picture tells my story and sheds light on my battle with Bulimia and where it all began.

Introduction

Bulimia. What does it look like? Frail? White? Dark circles around the eyes? Sunken cheeks? Blond hair? Blue eyes? Nope, not this time. Bulimia was me. A beautiful, black, intelligent, charismatic mother, sister, friend, and entrepreneur. Bulimia looked like me. Every time I ate, purged, and stared into the bathroom mirror, I was reminded that Bulimia resided within every corner and crevice of my mind reminding me of my painful past with each regurgitation. I was purging memories of my childhood, spiritual life, relationships and finances. Of course to the outside world, I looked as if I had it all together, or as one person said, "I was such a professional," but I knew the truth had to come out one day. Today is that day. Walk with me on my journey from Bulimic to Believer.

Caged Bird

Caged Bird you can fly,
The door is opened and you're free! Why are you still sitting in
that cage? You are able to fly wherever you see?

After being caged in for so long,
It's hard to imagine flying away from what has been home.
This cage has been all I've been able to fly around, coming outside
of it is fearful just to the sound.

Come to the edge just don't look down.
I'll put you on my shoulder and begin to carry you around.
You must come out the cage, you have been set free, Caged Bird,
trust me.

I'll come to edge and won't look down
You must promise to keep me safe and not allow me to fall down
to the ground.
The cage is so comfortable to me
The idea of being outside brings this overwhelming fear within me.

Just trust me, Caged Bird, I'll be right here, You're on my
shoulders, there's nothing to fear. For a while you'll go wherever I
go, then after seeing so much, you'll want to explore.
Even when you fly and explore I'll still be near, Because I've set
you free from all your fears.

The time has come for me to fly, all the promises you made none turned out to be a lie.
I've learned to trust you even when you said I can fly.
I'm spreading my wings and climbing high.
This flying isn't all as fearful as I imagined it would be.
I like the freedom to spread my wings and soaring as the wind carries me.
Thank you Mr. or Mrs., whomever you are, for seeing me
And knowing I would fly If only pushed to be free.

You're welcome, that's what I do.
I set Caged Birds free just like you.

This poem is dedicated to David & Beverly Sedlacek, and their ministry, *Into His Rest*. It has been through them and their team; JoAnne Palmer and Andrea Blackburn that Christ ascended from Heaven in human form and manifested Himself in my life. I am very grateful to have met and encountered them on my journey. They have labored with me through some of the dark places in my life never judging, but through it all pointing and directing me to the heart of Christ.

Acknowledgment

I am forever grateful that I was entrusted by the almighty God to write this book. It has been a journey to write it and at the same time, one that I felt unworthy of writing. I know and believe that I have been a conduit in which the Spirit used to get this new perspective of Bulimia to the world.

I'd like to thank all those who have been a part of this journey. My Heaven sent daughter, Jamiah Stroud, who has been a mirror reflecting back to me the image of myself. Because of her reflection, I saw and continue to see my heart issues that Christ wants to heal. She is my reason for writing. I didn't know I could write poetry until she showed me what she was learning while being home schooled.

To my parents Jimmy Stroud and Gaynell Tate, I wouldn't have life if it weren't for you. I thank you for coming alongside me during my process of counseling and being willing to see yourselves in relation to me. I couldn't have written this without your support and willingness to hear my truth no matter how ugly or messy it reflected you.

To my sister, Sherita Ware, thank you for coming alongside me in my counseling journey and being willing to get to the heart of the matter in our relationship so that we can truly say we love, understand, and support one another. We still have work to do, but we have begun the process of healing.

To my brother, Antonio Hill, your love and willingness to protect me as a young girl has never left my heart. You have and always will be a mighty man of God in my sight.

My beloved brother, Travor Reed, I simply love you to life and I couldn't have completed this book without you. Thank you for checking on me when everyone thought I was going crazy because I addressed my heart issues with dad.

There have been so many others who God has placed in my path that I am forever grateful for and if it had not been for them I don't know where I would be. My fourth grade teacher Mrs. White at Minor Elementary School, thank you for seeing something in me and telling me always I could do better. Mrs. Grizzel at

Ensley High School, thank you for not allowing me to settle with making a C because you knew a C wasn't my best work.

Pastor Willie Black, thank you for the real conversation and showing me that even though you were a pastor you were still a real person. You saw something in me when no one else in the church did. Thank you for drawing me out and allowing me to be me. I'm not sure who else Christ reached through you, but I believe you were sent just for me.

Pastor Albert Frazer, it was under your leadership that I first began to speak for Christ. Thank you for anointing me and allowing Christ to live in you even in the midst of your own crisis.

To David and Beverly Sedlacek, your book *Cleansing The Sanctuary of the Heart*, was life-changing and set my life on a new trajectory. I am forever grateful I met you all at a camp meeting; your ministry is Spirit-filled and Spirit-led. You and your team, JoAnne Palmer and Andrea Blackburn, have been trailblazing for me in discovering my purpose, passion and gaining a new perspective on life. I'm grateful and blessed to have and still be a part of your weekly conference calls and experience the retreats facilitated by you.

To my friends, LaTasha Brown Freeman, I couldn't have made it through summer 2015 without you going through it with me. You talked with me late night and early morning, you cried and brought laughter in the midst of my darkness, I love you to life. Wanda Johnson and Latoyia Wooden you both have put up with me even in the midst of shame when I left our friendship because of it, but you accepted me back. I have learned how to trust and love others for who they are and allow myself to be loved through my relationship with you ladies. It hasn't been smooth sailing, but through it all you all have been with me on the low road even when I pushed you all away I Love You.

To Bethany Seventh Day Adventist Church, thank you for being welcoming and accepting, you all embraced my daughter and I and loved us right where we were. With open arms and hearts, we were received and loved by you. Special thanks to Shanon Adedokun, for granting me comfort when I was in distress while at church by simply rubbing my back. To Tracey William thank you for seeing Jamiah and I as we are. Your willingness to sponsor Jamiah when I didn't have the funds brought me so much joy and I am very appreciative.

I couldn't have completed this book without Monique Nixon, the first editor and book coach. I knew you were God sent the day I spoke with you and you told me you were an editor. I said to God the day before speaking with you, "if I'm supposed to write a book I needed a scribe," and you showed up and were willing to do just that to get this message to the world. Thank you for putting up with me because I know it wasn't easy. I truly appreciate you.

For lack of space, to those who I didn't mention family and friends, I simply say thank you and I love you.

Shame to Free

Oh, the journey!
I've believed so many lies in between.
I believed I wasn't worthy of being truly happy because I viewed God as punishing me.

Punishing me for being bad, that's another lie that flowed and lived in my head. I understand you don't love me to hate me, because that type of love is slavery.

That type of love is driven by fear and in fear It's as if you're distant and not near.
It's oppressive and full of shame
That's the opposite of You, God, because freedom, liberation, and faith is Your name.

Shame, unworthiness, scared, and insecurity is green
Because the disgusted feeling they bring. I've been disgusted with the lies
I believed about myself and it's time to break free.

Anxiousness and the overwhelming feeling of living on the edge came along with the shame/fear team, but I'm no longer acquainted with you, it's time for me to move.

I believed the lie that I should be mediocre and small,
Because my greatness that You placed in me appeared to be too much for those around me.

I stopped dreaming for the stars and settled with just remaining small.
I wouldn't rock the boat and no one would notice me,
All the while screaming to be free.

I believed I failed at what You entrusted to me, Your precious child, who's also screaming to be free.
The business You gave to me is another, I felt like I failed due to my financial irresponsibility.

You didn't rob me of happiness,
I made a choice from the place I sat that happiness wasn't for me,
Because I had no clue it should be beautiful.

Forgiveness is what I need to do, for myself, to move from shame to free
And enter into Your rest of being able to just be me!
All of the lies I believed I renounce and accept Your truth that I am forgiven.

Precious, accepted, restored, understood, loved, free, worthy, grateful, redeemed, and safe with You. I'm even engraved in Your hand, You have never left me
And, I'm seen by You with all this stuff, You still see me as Beautiful.

Thank You for truly knowing second, third, and many more chances and having grace
When I'm not able to see, even then You carried and protected me.

Chapter 1
Bulimia A Different Perspective

Bulimia Nervosa can be described as noise and chaos within. It's a constant battle, or shall I say, a great controversy in the mind about a lie and the truth. Although some will know what bulimia looks like on the surface, the greater issue is within the heart. The mind of a bulimic was created in Genesis when Eve decided to believe the lie instead of the truth. The truth was Eve would experience death if she ate from the tree of the knowledge of good and evil, according to (Genesis 2:17) the lie told to Eve by the serpent was, "You shall not surely die." She subjected herself to listening to the outside noise, *"But the serpent said to the woman, you shall not surely die. For God knows that in the day you eat of it your eyes will be opened, and you will be like God, knowing the difference between good and evil and blessing and calamity."* (Genesis 3: 4-5 AMP).

The mind of a bulimic was created when he spoke and Eve listened which then created doubt. She acted on the doubt and shame that was birthed from her interaction with the serpent. Bulimia is a lie and shame. As we accept the lie, the inner turmoil begins, and the truth is fighting within to vindicate the lie, which leads to what we know as binging and purging or acceptance and rejection of the truth and lie.

We, like Adam and Eve, have a Genesis, or beginning. Our beginning is our childhood, and upon conception our great controversy, the noise began.

Noise, lies, and shame sound like this,

"You talk too much and ask too many questions," mentions the family friend.

"I'm coming to pick you up today," lies the non-custodial father.

"You shouldn't cut your hair because you don't look good with short hair," response from my maternal grandmother who has desired to have long hair as I did.

"You sure are pretty to be dark- skinned," voiced the lady at the grocery store.

"You are going to be pregnant before you turn 15," scowls the neighbor from across the street.

"You look like Celie from the movie *Color Purple*," says the sanctified church member.

"You only graduated with a 4.0 GPA because you went to Ensley High School," states the friend who went to one of the top five high schools in the state, Vestavia.

"What qualifications do you have to be the church clerk? You have to come before the nomination board and give a statement of your experience and qualifications," declares the elder member, who has married their position.

"You always want to go places where you're not wanted," frowns my only and eldest sister, whom I adore.

This noise in my head was hard to shake because I lived with it for so long. From all these experiences I heard and encountered, I felt as if I wasn't good enough and something was obviously wrong with me. After hearing and experiencing the noise, lies, and shame, I began to accept the lie as truth and acted out on what I heard and believed. All the lies and the noise became my truth.

Many Americans and people across the world suffer with this bulimic heart condition of noise, lies, and shame. Although they may not label their condition bulimia, it doesn't minimize the behavior that it leads to, a life conducive of death. Because I believed all the lies and carried all the shame, I didn't like my body and because of my self-hatred, I had a liposuction procedure on my thighs. I could've died on the table, in the clutter of noise drowned out by low self-esteem or no God-esteem, and self-hatred. I didn't value my body and see its worth because I was molested as a young girl, which lead to promiscuity. At the tender age of 13, I had contracted two sexually transmitted diseases, gonorrhea and herpes, which I thought was a death sentence. The God of my understanding was harsh and distant which further supported the lack of God-esteem.

At its damaging core, Bulimia Nervosa is an issue of the heart and mind. Curt Thompson, author of *Anatomy of the Soul*, says this, *"The heart is our deepest emotional/cognitive/conscious/unconscious self and is manifested most profoundly at the level of the prefrontal cortex."* The prefrontal cortex is within the brain. When I say the heart, I'm not referring to the vital organ that pumps blood, I'm referring to the central station of humanity, which involves the mind. The word heart, in the Bible, in many occurrences, is used metaphorically. The heart is referred to as the mind, emotions, or the will of the human nature. There are countless Scriptures that support this heart/mind idea. *"The heart is deceitful above all things, and it is exceedingly perverse and corrupt and severely, mortally sick! Who can know it [perceive, understand, be acquainted with his own heart and mind]? I, the Lord, search the mind, I try the heart, even to give to every man according to his ways, according to the fruit of his doings."* (Jeremiah 17:9-10

AMP) *"For the Word that God speaks is alive and full of power [making it active, operative, energizing, and effective]; exposing and sifting and analyzing and judging the very thoughts and purposes of the heart."* (Hebrews 4:12 AMP) *"He who leans on, trusts in, and is confident of his own mind and heart is a [self-confident] fool, but he who walks in skillful and godly Wisdom shall be delivered."* (Proverbs 28:26 AMP) There are others that reveal the idea, which supports the heart being the mind of man, (Psalms 26:2, Isaiah 29:13, Deuteronomy 30:17 AMP) to name a few.

Painful Truth

The attacks normally come from within,
within the boundaries of family and close friends.

Oh how hurtful and painful the attacks are, the reality is,
they are being who they are.

The words of your mouth pierce and cut even to the bone,
and they are dress up with "I'm concerned" and a low tone.

Not sure how my truth may offend you,
even though it doesn't involve you!

It's spoken and told so all who hear it will be
liberated to voice and speak their truth, too.

To those close, near or far, my truth will be spoken for God's
glory to draw
men, women, boy and girls across the world,
who has or is currently going through where I have been,
so they will know they're not alone, and they have an over-comer
as a friend.

Be liberated you are free!
Speak your truth
Because someone needs your truth too!

Chapter 2
Heart of The Matter

"Set up for yourselves highway markers, back to Cannan, make for yourselves guideposts; turn your thoughts and attention to way by which you went into exile. Retrace your steps...." (Jeremiah 31:21 AMP). My Canaan, the place flowing with milk and honey, was behind me, in my childhood, but it was also the place where things went terribly wrong. Here's the beginning of my life story.

I was about five years old but was not enrolled in school because I had a late birthday. My cousin and I were at my grandparent's house in Birmingham, Alabama. One fall morning we sat on the front porch with my grandfather. I remembered him sitting on the right side of the porch with an apple in one hand, and a spoon held tightly in the other. My grandfather was a tall man with a dark complexion. He had a habit of removing his dentures from his mouth while he ate, and today was no different. As I recall, it was very early in the morning, I can still vividly smell and see the early morning fog. It was also a brisk, cool morning and the leaves on the trees were changing colors. I watched my grandfather contently as he ate his apple. I instantly became elated, excited, and full of joy just to be there with him.

Later that day, my cousin and I were allowed to go across the street to play with our friend, Samantha. Samantha was short, chubby, and dark complexion with long ponytails. We ran up and down the hill in Samantha's yard as our grandfather watched us from his porch across the street. He would listen to us laugh and scream while having the time of our lives.

We would lie on the neatly cut lawn and I could feel the pricks of each blade of grass on my arms; some even could be felt through my sweaty clothes. We began to roll down the hill. We may have rolled individually or at the same time, but we rolled and rolled. As we rested at the top of the hill, the bottom appeared to be so very far away, but it didn't matter because we were having a great time just being carefree. Whenever we would tumble to the bottom, we would hop back up and run all the way back to the top, giggling and playing with one another. That last time we lay on the grass to roll, something felt very different. I felt as if my whole body was on fire. My lighthearted giggles instantly turned to piercing screams. There was pain all over my body from head to toe. By this time I noticed, my cousin was screaming too! My grandfather leapt from the porch as if he were a 27-year-old man, running fast across the street plucking us up from the yard. My cousin was hanging on for dear life under one arm, and I was screaming bloody murder while under the other. He turned toward his house and ran full speed ahead. I don't even remember him opening the door, but the next thing I knew we were in the bathtub. He dropped my cousin and I in the bathtub as if we were heavy potato sacks. We were in the bathtub fully clothed with ants floating gingerly in the water. My grandfather was frantic, his face flushed. Our screams subsided and his deep frown turned to a big grin. My grandfather was my hero that day. He was my hero every day.

One year later, I found myself standing at my mother's side, sobbing uncontrollably. There were sleek, black limos lined in formation outside of my grandparent's home, and I couldn't quite grasp the reason, but I understood that I was not going to see him anymore. My hero was gone. As the family cars started to line up, I was right by my mother's side, scared. The sobs became hysterical and because of this, I was the only child that rode in the first car with the adults. Silence permeated the air and all I could think about was my caped crusader would never return to rescue me from harm or danger ever again. I felt abandoned.

It was a sunny day when we arrived at the tiny church filled to capacity. There was an array of beautiful flowers at the front of it. I couldn't help but stare as we had to pass by them to get to our seat. We finally settled in our seats and before the eulogist could speak a word my eldest brother got up and ran out of the church. One of my uncles was very upset and he left in a hurry, too. My mother and other family members tried to catch my brother, but they were unsuccessful as they were upset also. The service continued and after my grandfather was in the ground, we returned back to my grandparent's home. I remember there were so many people in the house that day. Some were crying, others were laughing and talking loudly. I watched my grandmother from afar and she didn't shed a tear, not at the funeral and not at the house. Why didn't she cry? Was she not sad, or was she relieved that he was gone? I didn't understand and no one sat me down so I could gain an understanding of what happened. I was confused.

Two years later on a hot summer evening, my mom received a call. She immediately stopped what she was doing and rushed us out of the house. We rushed to the hospital, to be by my dad's side. His life was hanging in the balance because he had been shot and the bullet was lodged in the stomach. The reports from the doctor were not good and he was still in surgery. It didn't look as if he was going to live. My dad used and sold drugs, and his lifestyle was a contributing factor to him being shot, although his being shot wasn't directly related to his lifestyle. The doctor notified our family of the possible outcome as he prepared us to expect the worst. My paternal grandmother was there, so were my dad's siblings and others, all the people around were a blur, but there were several other people there. My mother was very close to God, or so I thought, because she was determined and adamant that God would heal him and my dad would survive. She prayed a lot, but I can't remember her crying, even though we were again faced with another painful moment in life.

There I was, this little girl faced with this fear of separation and abandonment again, with the possibility of losing another man whom I loved dearly. I didn't know what to feel. I don't remember crying this time. The tears didn't flow at all. I remember I paid close attention to all the adults, especially my mother. I observed her face so I could figure out how to feel. I watched her and I didn't see sadness, hurt, pain or fear; she appeared unbothered. Eventually he made it through surgery, but still had a long road to recovery. Although my dad didn't physically die, a part of him died on that table and it was very apparent. He remained in the hospital for well over a year during that time, I hated visiting him because he was in such a bad condition. He appeared to be helpless and I didn't want to see him that way. I learned to disconnect from that point and didn't truly feel what was going on within or around me. I was numb.

My grandfather was my rescuer and the apple of my eye because he provided emotional support and comfort that my dad wasn't able to provide. He was there for me when my father couldn't be, because as mentioned before, my father used drugs and wasn't very present in my home. About two or three years after my grandfather passed, and during the time my dad was in and out the hospital, I was molested by two males, a female family member, and an outsider. Molestation is being sexually assaulted or to make indecent sexual advancement without consent. As a young child, my innocence had been stolen from me.

The first violating experience took place at my grandparents' home, but the details are vague. The experience that haunted me for many years happened when I was eight or nine years old. My mother walked in the home and caught me sitting in the lap of one of my victimizers, a teenage family member. The living room was darker than a winter's night sky. He told me to sit on his wide lap as he placed my hand on his genitals. He then placed his hand on top of my hand and moved it in an up and down motion. I hated it, I felt degraded, disgusted, and violated, but I sat in fear and did it anyway because of the threats. "You better not say anything or you're going to get in trouble. If you say something they, aren't not going to believe you."

My mother walked in the house and immediately saw me sitting on his lap and asked no questions. She quickly called me into her room and screamed at me before she grabbed her extension cord. As she held the extension cord, she instructed my victimizer to hold both of my hands while his brother held my feet, I was confused again and I tried to explain what happened, but my mother wasn't listening and the lie was confirmed. They weren't going to believe me, and they didn't believe me because in that moment she proceeded to give me several lashes across my behind. My little mind couldn't quite grasp the reason why she was spanking me. What did I do wrong? Not only did I feel bad physically, but mentally, I was hurt. Why was she mad at me? Why wasn't she mad at him, too? I didn't understand what I had done to deserve this abuse, but understanding didn't comes until many years later, not that I deserved the whipping, but the reason behind my mother's reaction. I was feeling pained.

Two years later while my family and I lived in the projects, it happened again. Our neighbors, a nice family, had an older teenage male living with them. I was still in elementary school during the time he sexually assaulted me. This memory is a bit hazy; I don't remember all the details. We were playing a game in the living room and there was a plush, dark blanket on the living room floor. I lay down on the blanket and the next thing I remember, my mom was driving me to the hospital in silence. I sat in the icy, white room stone faced. My mom was right by my side when the tall, male Caucasian physician entered the room. He told my mom my tests were negative as there was no penetration. He then turned to me and said, "This is not your fault. There was nothing you could do that would have changed what happened."

His blue eyes met my dark brown eyes to assure me everything was okay. We stared at one another for a brief second before my mom let out a big sigh and a look of relief flashed across her face and broke our steadfast trance. This somehow brought me comfort, because my mother didn't show emotions. She was emotionless when my grandfather passed, when my father was shot, and when she whipped me after she caught one of my molesters. For some reason after I saw that emotion, I felt safe and secure. We went to Milo's after the incident and ate our meal in silence. I never visited Milo's again during my childhood, teenage years, and part of my adult years because of the negative memory associated with that restaurant. The next time I ate at Milo's was in 2013 with my daughter, mother, and younger cousin as I gained new and positive memories. We ate together as I shared the initial experience at Milo's with them.

Dancing was the creative expression I loved. At the age of thirteen, the movements stopped. The summer of my 8th grade year, I really wanted to dance. I asked my mother if I could be a part of this dance group that some friends belonged to. My mom was busy with work and didn't have time to check the group out, but heard the excitement in my voice as I persisted with my inquiries. I got the green light and joined the dance team. The team was organized and managed by two older black men. There was no cost to join this team.

Our first show was at a nightclub. We were the backup dancers for a struggling rap group. As I entered the dark nightclub, I immediately knew this didn't feel right. I and two other girls, were given black biker shorts and matching crop tops and told by the older men to change into this particular outfit.

There was a high school boy on the team that was nice looking and my thirteen-year-old self liked the attention I was getting from him. One sunny summer day, he asked to come over and I agreed. I was home alone which was normal because my mom was at work. He came over and we went into the room I shared with my sister. After he was there for a while, we sat on my twin bed. I remember him lying me down as he began to fondle me. I hated it and mentally left the room in the process.

Two weeks later we went on a family trip to Six Flags Over Georgia. It was a hot day. I wore a yellow shirt and a red, yellow, and blue Tommy Hilfiger outfit. My hair was slicked back in a ponytail with a pair of White Air Force Ones. I looked great on the outside, but something was going on within me. Walking and sitting became very painful. I pushed through the pain and had fun. I told my mom what I was experiencing and we went to the doctor the next day.

I sat in the room in silence with my mom by my side. The doctor came in I explained what I was experiencing, and told me he needed a urine sample, which I provided. I walked for what seemed like a mile to the restroom and through the pain I provided the sample. My walk back seemed even longer. The doctor explained he had to do a vaginal exam and what the process would be. I removed my bottoms while my mother sat in the room with me and covered myself up with the sheet. The doctor processed the exam and I felt so ashamed, although I was receiving the help I needed. I got dressed and we waited in silence for the doctor's return. He returned and began to speak to my mom, I sat and listened, but it was as if I wasn't in the room. He explained to my mom that I had contracted Gonorrhea and Herpes. He gave her a prescription to be filled and told her when I should take it. I watched my mom and I saw the shame all over her. I didn't know what either of these were at the time, but I know it wasn't good news.

The drive home was silent. My mom got the prescription filled and we didn't say a word to each other. I had questions and wanted to know what was going on with me, but she had no answers. I was told to tell my siblings when I got home what the doctor said and I did. I was left with questions, thoughts and feelings without answers. A part of me died that day and the dancing for expression completely stopped. There was so much shame associated with this because I didn't get answers and understanding about Herpes and what it meant until winter of 2015, the very thought of it made me want to throw up because I did not have an understanding. From that day forward, I began to pray for healing, and unbeknownst to me, my life's purpose would come through these experiences as a minister of healing.

The molestation and promiscuity left me feeling out of control, as if I had, "property of others" stamped on my forehead. It made me feel as if everyone had complete control over me, to do what they wanted, when they wanted. With every loss, I didn't gain an understanding nor did I know how to process my feelings. I learned by watching the adults and their emotions, or lack thereof, that crying and talking about my feelings was not the answer. With all the pain I witnessed and experienced, I never saw anyone cry or talk about their pain. The assaults and molestation lead me down a very dark and destructive path having a ton of emotions and not knowing how to process them. Because of this very reason, I began to binge and purge as a remedy for my internal pain.

Body Captivity

"Don't judge her! You don't know her story and you don't know the things she has been through."

"She's too darn fast, she'll be pregnant before she turns 15, and she's a freak." I've heard these words far too many times about young girls who are promiscuous. But guess what? No one has sat down with her to hear her story, to understand how she got to those places and behavior that she's in.

If you knew her, you would know that several family members molested her. Her innocence, choice and childhood had been stolen from her. Her personal boundaries had been crossed, and now she feels as if she's worthless, useless, and damaged goods. Her body is now community property, because if one, two, or three people did what they wanted with her body, does she have any say? Her ability to say no had been confiscated. She lives in captivity within her own body. Something was taken from her and now the violating path has been laid down in her brain while she continues to allow others to take a part of her.

Every time she was violated, a part of her is scattered and left with the person. Every time she lay there, it was just as violating as the first time because she hadn't healed from her pain. There may be different faces, but the experience is the same-painful, violating, and degrading. It hurts her to hear what others are saying about her and she wants to stop, but the story (lie) in her head tells her that she has no hope and she believes the lie.

Until she began to come to herself, wanting to be free from her own body captivity. One day, five years ago, she took a vow for celibacy and searched for counseling because she was destined to be free. She read a text that spoke to her soul and gave her hope that she can be whole. "And I will bring you out from the people and will gather you out of the counties in which you are scattered, with a mighty hand and an outstretched arm and with wrath poured out." (Ezekiel 20:34). That text spoke to her and she interpreted it to mean that she would be gathered from all the sexual violating places she had been scattered about, and it would be done with a mighty hand just for her.

Did I mention "she" was me? Thank God He stepped in my story to release me from the body captivity?

Chapter 3
Food Addict

I became pregnant at the age of 19 and this was a bad experience for me emotionally. Food became comfort for me. Food was comfort before my pregnancy. I realized how much food was comfort when I became pregnant. I gained an unusual amount of weight during and after the pregnancy. I was heavier than what I was used to being. This was the beginning of my conscious issues with food and weight. Although I wasn't purging during my pregnancy, I was binge eating.

As I mentioned in the previous chapter, I watched the adults in my childhood handle pain without any expression, so I learned to do the same. The binging and purging of food became a way of expressing my feelings. This is what's described as emotional eating. Every time I felt overwhelmed, out of control, fear, shame, happy, or excited, I ate a lot of food. Shortly afterwards, the guilt from consuming so much would creep in, and I would throw it up, or purge. I not only binged and purged the negative emotions; I did the same with positive emotions because I didn't know how to express either. I was cold.

All my friends around me were about the same size and we teased, or shall I say, shamed one another about our weight all the time. One day, one of my friends decided she wanted to do something different so she began a journey to lose weight and was very successful. I wasn't in the place where I wanted to make a change for my life, so I watched her from the sideline as she pursued her goals. The weight began to shed and I noticed and others began to notice as well. I was very competitive by default and when I realized people took notice of her and her weight loss, I became very envious and wanted to lose weight, too.

I was 22 years old when the weight loss journey began. I remember going to the gym five days a week for 30 minutes in the beginning, then that soon turned to five days a week twice a day for an hour or two or three. I was in excess mode. I shifted focus from my friend, and focused my journey on a girl's trip to Miami. In January, I set a target weight of 150 pounds and I was willing, unbeknownst to me, to subject my body to intense pain and torture.

The moment I began to binge and purge my food is a blur, but I recall feeling really full and unsettled within even when I didn't eat that much. I felt as if the food I ate wasn't digesting and it was stuck in my throat, so one day I decided to assist my body. I went to the bathroom, got on my knees, and placed my hand in my mouth. I began to heave a couple of times then the flood of food came rushing into the toilet. I saw chunks of food I ate and could identify each and every thing I consumed. Suddenly, I felt relieved. I didn't feel full anymore and what appeared to be stuck in my throat was removed. I was empty and cherished this feeling because it felt way better than being "stuffed" or full. It was a very daunting progression or shall I say slippery slope, because I found myself spiraling out of control. Then, I started my fascination with laxatives. I started with one a day to completely empty myself of what I couldn't purge.

Over the next 5-6 year period, I moved up from one to five laxatives a day. I continued going to the gym day in and day out as I worked out despite fatigue and exhaustion. The laxatives would have my body hurled over in pain as I would wake at 3:00 am to eliminate excess food and weight. This was a daily cycle that I was in because I was going through a very dark period in my life. I embraced the darkness so much in my life that I even contributed to it by placing a blanket over my window so no sunlight would enter my room.

Here's an example: It is 3:00 am in the morning and the pain in my stomach is unbearable. I felt as if my stomach was on the spin cycle of the washing machine. I felt as if something was ripping my intestines from the inside out. The laxatives had begun working and I couldn't bear the pain. I crawled out of bed and stumbled to the bathroom while clasping my stomach.

I hurriedly turned on the light and sat down quickly on the cold toilet seat. I waited for what seemed like an eternity and nothing came out, but the pain was very intense. The pain made me move from the toilet to the floor as I laid there clenching my teeth and gripping my stomach while curled into a fetus position. I remembered I didn't shed one tear. I couldn't cry because I learned as a little girl not to shed a tear, even in pain. The pain was so unbearable, but I still couldn't cry so I lay there for about two hours staring at the back of my eyelids until I felt the release coming. I crawled back to the toilet and began to release all the food that I wasn't able to purge from the previous purging session. It was a bittersweet moment; the pain was now gone and I felt relieved, but the next day I did it all over again, because the release was temporary.

The shame and guilt was so heavy that I didn't tell anyone so I suffered in silence, as my body seemed to be wasting away. As a little girl, I learned that people would judge and criticize me if I told them what was going on. I didn't want to open myself up to ridicule and torture by the people who were supposed to love and be there for me. I felt like nothing, a complete waste of space and body. So what did I do? I put on a happy face, hid my emotions, and kept right on with life, as I knew it.

It's interesting that those around me saw this young professional, confident, outgoing female who appeared to love herself. I'm very outgoing and could hold a conversation with anyone, but to truly encounter me at that place and moment in time, one would sense something was going on within. I was very harsh and judgmental of others; this was a defense to keep people from getting close and really knowing my heart issues. Let me be clear, this wasn't something I was conscious of at the time; I discovered this after going through intense counseling sessions.

At events and gatherings, I appeared to be so controlled with my eating habits that people rarely noticed. I only ate a small amount in public to avoid having to purge while others were around and notice my behavior. I was very good at hiding my symptoms and disease or so I thought, but once I got home, it was on and popping. As I drove home, the anxiety and anticipation of purging would be so intense because I couldn't wait to get home to rid myself of what I ate. I couldn't just go to sleep with food inside my stomach. I had to release. One time I remember walking into my kitchen after a party, rummaging around in my pantry until I found what I was looking for. I laid eyes on the food and my mind screamed, "Jackpot!" There were three packs of two count Nutty Bars lying in the cabinet. I ran to the couch and ate them one by one. I bit each layer individually as if I were performing surgery. I ate all three in silence and secrecy, but yet I still wasn't satisfied. My mind began to race as I decided to turn on the faucet in the kitchen and drink water directly from the spigot. I wanted to fill my stomach with water until I burst. Yes, I hated that "full" feeling, but this was exactly what I needed to purge. I finally rushed to the bathroom, got on my knees, stuck my hand inside my mouth and touched the back of my throat until that warm rush of liquid passed my waiting tongue and plopped into the toilet. I was in pain, but also felt a rush of relief, or so I thought. I got up, wiped my mouth, and proceeded to take more laxatives. After I finished my shower, it was off to bed so I could wake up and do it all over again. It was truly sad, I looked forward to the next day, but I also dreaded it, too, because I had to do it all over again. The vicious, tumultuous cycle would take over me more. Food was the drug of choice. I hid, binged, and purged so much until I hit rock bottom and landed flat on my face.

My view of self was severely distorted; the shame was so intense I wasn't able to see anything clearly. I went from 210 to 135 pounds within a few months. My chest, neck, and ribs were visible and I believed I was still fat. I would go out to the clubs and loved the attention I got, but it still wasn't enough. When looking in the mirror I saw an ugly, fat, black girl. I was unlovable, unlikeable, and uninteresting. I never saw myself as beautiful even though others told me I was. My perception of me didn't let me see or hear it. Right before I began to lose weight, I consulted with a plastic surgeon about cosmetic surgery; liposuction on my thighs, to be exact. I hated my thighs. All my life I have been shapely and received a lot of attention on my lower body; I despised such attention and did whatever I could to hide it.

I met with a plastic surgeon in Birmingham, AL at the Kirklin Clinic. He advised me to lose weight before I had surgery and I successfully achieved what the doctor ordered. I lost weight by any means necessary. After I lost weight, I went back about a year and a half later yet still unsatisfied. I wanted smaller thighs. I consulted with the doctor again. I scheduled the surgery and went through the procedure. After the procedure was performed, I was still ashamed because I didn't want anyone to know what I had done. One day after I had recovered from the procedure, I realized my right thigh was slightly bigger than the left, and I'm stuck to this present day with one thigh slightly bigger than the other.

Due to shame and bulimia I felt worthless and out of control on the inside, my beauty would still seem to radiate on the outside.

March of 2014 I sat in my office located in Homewood, Alabama, with my employee, Blana. A client walks in and appears to be Hispanic, or so I thought. He was interested in having his taxes prepared. I was at the front desk so I called Blana to the front for her to assist him with his return, because I don't speak Spanish. Blana comes up and talks with him and escorts him to her desk.

Blana called my name, "Jamella?"

"Yes," I replied.

"Can you come to my desk, please?" She politely asked.

The gentlemen seated at her desk asked, "Your name is Jamella?"

"Yes"

He said it again, "Jamella?"

I began to feel strange and awkward because I wondered what was really going on and the reason behind him stating my name repeatedly. The stranger noticed that I was uncomfortable so he then stated, "Where I'm from, when we call someone Jamella, we are calling them beautiful, your name means beautiful."

My confused face turned into the biggest smile, as I inquired where he was from.

"Jerusalem," He stated boldly. My smile became bigger.

I was so very excited to hear this. It was much needed in my life at that point in time. I was on a downhill spiral and about to lose it all. I later asked my mother the origin of my name and how she came up with it. She stated, "I'm not sure how it happened," but at that moment I was glad she did. My whole life I felt ugly, but God had been calling me beautiful the entire time. I no longer wanted to be called, "Mella" as my childhood friends and family called me. I only wanted to answer to Jamella from then on. I wanted to be called Jamella because I embraced my beauty within. I was reminded of my Creator's words, *"Before I formed you in the womb I knew [and] approved of you [as My chosen instrument], and before you were born I separated and set you apart, consecrating you; [and] I appointed you as a prophet to the nations."* (Jeremiah 1:5 AMP)

What I later learned is bulimia was connected to family losses, molestation, and promiscuity. All the unreleased emotions from childhood associated with these events. Bulimia was more about control, rejection, abandonment, and shame than weight loss. As I mentioned in Chapter 2, with the family loss and molestation, I felt as if I had no control over what happened to me. I felt as if I lost all power and my body was the pleasure playground for victimizers leaving me without a choice. One day the connection came together and it began to make sense.

On a humid, July, Sunday evening my maternal family met to play Pokeno. We gathered together to play this game every Sunday. This particular Sunday we were at the home of one of my molesters. I played the game and it was going well, or so I thought, until I actually sat on what felt like an ice cold chair at the square table. I felt my concentration fleeting, my focus was scattered, my hands began to shake and things began to blur. What's going on I thought to myself, why can't I focus? I felt scared, fear was all over me and I couldn't play the game. My heartbeat accelerated and my breath became shorter. I was frozen in fear. I said to my mother as she sat beside me, "I don't know what's going on, but I can't focus." She didn't say anything, as she did in childhood, so I played the remainder of that game, unable to be fully present in the moment, and then I left to go home. As soon as I arrived home, I went to my "darkroom" and fell to my knees. "Lord, help me! I can't do this anymore." I cried out as tears scurried down my cheeks. "I don't know what's going on with me, but I can't take it any longer."

My prayer was sincere and true. In that moment, the pieces began to come together and I began to connect the experience dots. I was in the very space of my victimizer and although I had been in his presence before, this time was different, all the years I told myself I was fine and the molestation didn't bother or affect me began to fall down on me like an avalanche. The ice was melting from my heart and my emotions were rushing down my slope. If I were a skier, I would have been buried under the ice as I tried to out ski my emotional avalanche. To my dismay, I could no longer run from my emotions. *"Set up for yourselves highway markers back to Canaan, make for yourselves guideposts; turn your thoughts and attention to the way by which you went into exile. Retrace your steps..."* (Jeremiah 31:21 AMP) Highway markers are what we used on the expressway or roads to tell us what direction we are headed in, and how far we are from the desired location. Canaan was the Promised Land, the place flowing with milk and honey for the children of Israel. God tells them to turn their thoughts and attention backwards, because they were, at the time, headed into captivity and the answer to where they were, how they got to that place, and where they were going was behind them.

Why did I feel the need to be in control, one might ask? I felt as if I had lost control through my past experiences. I found myself as a bulimic, due to what happened in my land flowing with milk and honey, or my childhood. The weight had become something that I thought I could control, but I didn't realize that very thing I thought I had under control was very much controlling me. This avalanche was flowing full speed ahead and I was not quite ready.

The Breakup

The day I met you, I can't recall,
our initial introduction is like the fog.

Oh, I remember my family introduced me to you.
Upon introduction, I immediately didn't like you.

I didn't like how I felt when you were around.
I would withdraw and pretend to be small,
and disappear because I felt the fear.

Other times you were near me,
I would lash out and fight for,
what appeared to be, my sanity.
Oh my, you have never been good for me!

We have known each other for far too long
and this thing we have is as a thorn.

It hurts and is painful, even the very thought of you.
I realize this relationship I can no longer do.

I'm so done and over you.
I allowed you to stick around for far too much time,
And it has drained, stained, and corroded me on the inside.

Who are you? What's your name?

I'm breaking up with you,
FEAR, ABANDONMENT, REJECTION, and SHAME!

Chapter 4
Emotional Roller Coaster

When I felt "out of control" emotionally, I would try to gain control of something externally and this was done by binging and purging. This is the one thing I thought I had under control.

I grew up with this tainted trash can of unresolved emotional issues, the loss of my grandfather, my dad being shot, molestation, promiscuity and sexually transmitted diseases were all stuffed and the stench was seeping out. I didn't have a template or owner's manual on how to express these feeling of shame, abandonment, rejection, and victim, which said to me, I'm wrong, I'm not enough, what happened to me was my fault, I'm bad, I'm unworthy, and I had no power over anything that happened in my life.

The physical manifestation of bulimia was indicative of my emotional state. When I felt all these things, I would get physically full as this matched my emotional fullness. I didn't know how to express these emotions in a healthy way; therefore, I would purge and feel a false sense of release. This release was false because I hadn't dealt with the foundation or root of my issue, not knowing at the time bulimia was the effect, but the real issues were yet to be known. The Bible says, *"So we fix our eyes not on what is seen, but on what is unseen, since what is seen is temporary, but what is unseen is eternal."* (2 Corinthians 4:18NIV). I suggest bulimia is truly an unseen issue and what we see, the binging and purging, taking laxatives, fasting, and over exercising stems from a place of emotional toxicity. Treatment and prevention must be dealt with from within. I continued this vicious cycle day in and out in an attempt to release and find comfort for the brokenness within.

I learned from the various traumatic experiences not to talk about what was going on inside. As a child, I didn't see the adults in my life having conversations about their feelings relating to painful events. My mother did the best she could do with what she had. She gave me what she had emotionally. Learning and understanding my beliefs, thoughts and feelings that sent me to binging and purging behavior was imperative to my healing; until that pinnacle was reached, a breakthrough healing was highly unlikely.

REJECTION

I was at a new place, new job, and city. No family to depend on and no friends that I knew. The president at my job told me I could go back to my business, because I spoke out about things that were unhealthy on the job. I wondered and asked God, "Why did you allow me to move away from all that is comfortable to me, to bring me to a place where I felt rejected and condemned for speaking out?" I later discovered moving and experiencing rejection was apart of the plan to heal the pain of feeling rejection.

On the way home one night from work, I felt extremely tired and overwhelmed. The workload was astounding and I dreaded the 1 hour and 30 minute drive back home to Moody, Alabama. As I drove down the highway with these mass emotions rumbling about in my head, I decided to pullover and get something to eat because I didn't want to miss dinner as it was getting late. I hastily ate my meal and with the last bite, I immediately felt shame rear its ugly head. I fought tirelessly with this battle and contemplated pulling the car over on the expressway and purge. I had been in counseling an entire year. Therefore I knew purging was not an option, but I still had the feeling that I needed to purge. I couldn't shake it.

Instead of pulling over, I frantically looked for my phone and called my sister.

"Hey, I feel like I want to purge, I feel like pulling the car over and purging. I'm not sure what's going on or why I'm feeling like this." The words spewed from my mouth a mile a minute. She asked, "What happened today at work?" Without even thinking about my response I began to ramble, "I was really busy and the workload is way too much, I'm doing the job of at least three people and I'm exhausted. I also went to the Executive Director and told him of my interest with working with Family Ministry and I was told they have someone in mind that's getting a doctorate to oversee the department. "My sister recognized the anxiety in my voice, "Jamella, breathe. Take some deep breaths. How did that make you feel?"

Her voice was very soothing. I continued talking, "I'm not sure how it makes me feel, but I don't like it." "What does he mean, and why did he need to tell me this?" I was not only livid, but I felt a myriad of different emotions in the pit of my stomach. I was frustrated as I answered this question. I exhaled and inhaled long, deep breaths before it hit me. I felt rejected and unworthy! The rejection within sent me to a place where I accepted (binged), then rejected (purged). I wept as I felt the impact from the morbid feeling of rejection, and I wept until it was all out of my system.

Binge eating occurs when one eats, but isn't mindful of the amount of what he or she is eating. As you notice in the above story, I ate the food while driving and multitasking. This means I wasn't fully engaged in the consumption of the food. When I finished eating, I felt worse than I had before. This sent me into deeper shame, and I was headed into a downward spiral to begin purging, but before I went to the other extreme I became mindful. I needed to release those emotions, but I knew in my head purging wasn't going to give me what I needed, I relied on my past experiences. The conversation and weeping became purging and it also got to the root cause of the true issue, rejection and feelings of unworthiness.

In *Anatomy of the Soul*, by Curt Thompson, M.D, he stated, *"The constant monitoring and shifting in energy is the activity around which the brain organized itself. This is emotion. The origin of our world is grounded in the idea of e-motion, or preparing for motion. That is why the phenomenon of emotion is deeply tied to ongoing action or movement. We cannot separate what we feel from what we do."*

Because we can't separate what we feel from what we do, I felt rejected. Rejection was my emotion, and I wanted to act out that emotion through purging. The feeling of rejection is at the very core of a bulimic. These emotions ran deep and the issue must be dealt with at the root of where it began.

ENRAGED

I was invited to a retreat and all week I kept telling myself I wasn't going, but for some reason I was destined to be there. My sister and I were traveling by car. She was on the phone and I asked her if I could speak with our friend to inquire about a couples mini retreat her cousin was hosting. My sister sneered, "Why do you always try to go places you're not wanted? You're not coming to our couples gathering." Boy, did I let her have it. I screamed at her to the top of my lungs. I glanced into the rearview mirror as my daughter sat wide-eyed, stunned as she witnessed this fiasco take place right before her eyes. Later on, my daughter said she thought I was going to cry, but I didn't, at that moment I know I had needed to go to the Keys Emotional Healing Retreat. I asked God to show me the true issue behind my anger. At that moment I had a toxic rupture, I totally disintegrated and my amygdale, the seat of emotions within the brain, was in total control, as expressed by Curt Thompson in *Anatomy of the Soul*.

RELIEF

At the Keys to Emotional Healing retreat facilitated by three amazing women who has inspired and mentored me, my trailblazers Beverly Sedlacek, JoAnne Palmer, and Andrea Blackburn, I learned about my rejection issues. I had over the past month, been in several situations where I had the same feeling, but I wasn't sure what it was. One thing's for sure I didn't like it and I couldn't understand it until the retreat. I explained all of the above situations and through them God revealed and allowed me to have an experience with him where I went back to the place of rejection.

January 17, 2015 was the day I received a breakthrough and revelation. I sat on the couch at the retreat and cried, but I was still unaware of the source of my tears. Beverly comes over to sit next to me and asked if she could pray, to which, I replied, "Yes."

She gently stated, "Can Jesus come and minister to you where you are?"

Through my tears, I again said yes.

I continued to cry, and then I went to a safe place in my head and thought about water. Water has always been my safe place, although, I didn't know that until this moment. I saw myself as an adult sitting in a tube of water in the fetus position. Then I went back to being a little girl between the ages of 5-6 years old in an old home in Ensley, Alabama. I came out of my room to go to my mom's room, but the door was closed. I was locked out of the very place I wanted to be: in my mom's room and in her heart. I stood there in my tears, not able to get in.

Beverly interrupted my thoughts and reiterated the question, "Can Jesus come to you at the place you are right now?"

Sobbing, I replied, "Yes."

At that very moment I saw Jesus. A bright light appeared around Him as He grabbed my hand and walked me back to my room. Jesus tucked me into the covers on my bed and kissed my forehead. At that point, my physical body was still curled up in a fetal position on Beverly. I was sweating profusely while shaking and weeping hysterically. Jesus spoke to me and said, *"I accept you. I love you, rest my child."* I was later informed that I didn't stop shaking until He stated that last part, "Rest my child."

After this touching experience, I was depleted, exhausted, and void of energy. The smell of food made me sick to my stomach and I had diarrhea. They allowed me to stay in the living room on the couch for the rest of the day. Later that night about 8:30pm, I sat in the hot tub to regroup because my body was aching from such an emotional experience. Shame set in after rejection was released. They saw me, and I felt naked and my separation from the group was due to my shame of being seen. This caused my layers and flaws to be exposed. The next day I woke up refreshed and rejuvenated.

Upon coming home from the retreat, I mentioned to my mother about the whole experience. I revealed how I saw myself in water curled up in a fetal position. I talked about my discovery of the root of my fear of rejection and the other issues that came with it. I also inquired about her pregnancy experience with me. My mother explained to me that she didn't initially want me when she found out she was pregnant. Before she became pregnant with me, she had an abortion because she didn't want any more children. She said she felt as if she was being punished when she became pregnant with me. The root of my rejection issues lay within me in-utero. This explained a lot. My mother rejected me in-utero, my father wasn't excited about my birth, and my father's mother even questioned if I were his child. Imagine growing up even before birth with a weight of rejection hovering over your life, even before I knew who I was, I struggled with this heavy burden.

Rejection is described as a constant feeling of loneliness and isolation, not being able to accept what is. If the very people who created me rejected me, how would I know acceptance? My Creator was acquainted with my feelings. We are told, *"He was despised and rejected and forsaken by men, a Man of sorrows and pains, and acquainted with grief and sickness; and like One from Whom men hide their faces He was despised, and we did not appreciate His worth or have any esteem for Him."* (Isaiah 53:3 AMP) I went through life not truly feeling accepted and not truly accepting others until the age of 32.

ACCEPTANCE

That same year, the day after Christmas, I must say I had an awesome time at church. I knew within my heart Christ was with us. My mom came to church with me and I was very excited, because she drove to where I lived. I wasn't sitting with her for most of church, because I was out with a member's son in the nursery. My mother allowed herself to have an experience with God that day, too. I truly felt like a little kid, because my mom accepted me. The very place and person where my rejection issues began, through her, God gave me another experience to change that feeling. It was the first time I really felt accepted for who I am and I began to accept myself for who I am and was created to be.

As a gift, my mom purchased a tube of lipstick, Instigator, by Mac Cosmetics for me. Well, this was, is, a big deal for me because I grew up in a really strict Seventh Day Adventist church, and my outward appearance was heavily focused on. I proudly wore the lipstick she purchased for me to church because my mother purchased it. Later that evening, my mother said she wanted to hold me. I can't recall a time where my mom just held me although I longed for that moment. I lay on my bed with my legs and feet slightly bent, and she laid behind me with hers arms around my waist. I took deep breaths and stayed in that moment as I truly felt accepted, just as I was. The lipstick still freshly painted on my lips, my mother didn't try to change me, but she allowed me to just be me in her presence.

Divide

*I'm spent, exhausted, beat
my head and heart feels like two separate beats!*

Beat, thump, click, clock!

*Over thinking, analyzing, head stop!
Give up, let go!
What exactly are you trying to control?*

*The beat of your heart, the thing you don't want to feel.
This place you can't think your way through,
you must let go and feel to deal.*

*The two separate beats one say feel the other say think.
Letting go and feeling doesn't come easy for me,
but with you what's not easy for me you'll see me
through.*

*I'm weary and my soul crying out for you,
make these two beats meet and beat for you!*

*Lord, God, Savior, Friend, Comforter, Almighty,
Ruler, King, Father, Redeemer, Hope, Faith!*

*My heart yearns for you to touch me in that place,
you created for you and only you!*

Chapter 5
Financial/Business Bulimia

"Honor your father and your mother, as the Lord your God commanded you, that your days may be prolonged and that it may go well with you in the land which the Lord your God gives you." (Deuteronomy 5:16 AMP).

Due to a lack of honor and judgments for my mother in the financial area, I too, had difficulty in the same area even though I thought I was doing something different. *"Do not judge and criticize and condemn others, so that you may not be judged and criticized and condemned yourselves. For just as you judge and criticize and condemn others, you will be judged and criticized and condemned, and in accordance with the measure you [use to] deal out to others, it will be dealt out again to you."* (Matthew 7:1-2 AMP)

At the age of 27, I started a tax preparation business. As a young child, I knew I would be an entrepreneur, but my dream was quite different; I dreamed of having a law firm. I witnessed my brother receive 21 years as a first time offender for robbery. I felt the strict consequences were not fair as it outweighed the crime. My desire was to help others like him. After completing my four years of college, I headed to law school. My daughter was five years old at the time and I remember the car ride that changed the trajectory of my life.

CHANGE IS GOOD

The day was long and exhausting. I had just left law school and picked up my daughter, Jamiah, and headed home. As we drove through the parking lot of Winn Dixie, about a block from the apartment, Jamiah began a conversation with me.

"Mom, she asked from the backseat, "do you have to study tonight?"

"No," I replied.

"Do you have to do homework?" She probed again.

"No." I stated again while glancing back at her through my rear-view mirror.

She took a deep breath and sighed, "Finally, we can spend some time together."

In that moment I knew I had to do something different, I had been there for her, or so I thought. I was home every night, I clothed her with the best money could buy, made sure she ate, we even played some games together now and then, so what did she really mean? I realized even though I was doing all that stuff, I wasn't emotionally available for her and my reality was I didn't know how to be there. I could only give her what I had gotten and as we discovered in previous chapters, my parents were not emotionally available for me. I ventured to do something different. I left law school in hopes to change my relationship with her and be more available, although this was unsuccessful, because I didn't have a template for what that looked like.

I had the opportunity to work for a small income tax preparation business, as the receptionist and a tax preparer. I was eager to learn the field so I decided to take some courses that would equip me to do the job, because knowing and understanding why a client received a certain refund was just as or more important than knowing how to complete the return. Also, the idea of not completing an accurate return terrified me.

My time there was brief and short lived. I worked from December 2008 until February 2009. I was always a fast learner, when I paid attention. When I left I knew what I had to do to open my own business. I purposed in my mind and heart to open this business so I could be available for my daughter and still have financial freedom; well at least that's what I thought. I later discovered the business was also a contributor to the bulimic behavior.

The first year in operational business was 2010 and I was determined to get it started. I worked as a shampoo technician at my friend's salon and used the money I earned there to fund my business. I was on section 8 and was receiving food stamps at the time. However, money was available and I thought I could do as I pleased and I did, even then I was purging my finances.

I wasn't sure how I would get the necessary equipment to start the business during the year, but I continued to move forward with opening. In December of 2009, my mother gave me $300.00. I also applied for a business credit card for one of the office stores and was approved for $1000.00. I was able to purchase all I needed to start business. I rented a small space in the salon and many of the initial clients came from there. In January of 2010, I opened for business, making roughly $25,000 from January to March. I continued to work for the salon after the season because I wanted a location the next tax season. I had never made $25,000 so quickly and this was a huge amount of money for me to have obtained in such a short period of time. I was excited about this and I knew this was the business for me.

How does this relate to bulimia? Well bulimic behavior would have one to binge, consume an excess amount of food, and later purge by regurgitation, or take laxatives to eliminate that "full" feeling. This was my first business/financial binge. I gathered the excess amount of money in a short period of time and I purged/ spent it all throughout the year without any thought or plan as to where it was going. Even though I worked to obtain it, I felt ashamed. I felt as if I was wrong for having it in the first place. This is the same exact feeling I would get when I would eat excessively and get rid of it by purging. I had started something even though I felt ashamed with the money, I would purge and feel even more ashamed without it; my worth was attached to it. As with food I would do it all over again in hopes that the next time I would do something different.

MORE MONEY, MORE PROBLEMS

By the beginning of the next tax season I obtained a storefront location and was determined to do business bigger and better. Because I wasn't paying attention to what I was doing, things happened the same way even though I thought I was doing something different.

I called an old co-worker who previously worked with me at a kids clothing store a few years prior. I thought she would be a great fit for the business even though we had issues in the past. Though we were different in race, our stories were similar, I asked if she would be interested in being the office manager and we discussed pay. Shortly thereafter she joined the team. Not only did I employ her I employed two receptionist and two preparers. I didn't have an actual business plan, but I planned to make as much money as I could due to the fact that I was broke by the end of year one, and I believe that if I had more money, I wouldn't have that issue in year two. By the end of the tax season the business grossed about $87,000. Of course I was excited and felt accomplished. Since there was no separation of the two entities, the business, and myself I felt that *I* made the $87,000 and I functioned in that manner. I had another successful binge and I acquired this money very quickly and just as the year before it was fleeting. *"Like the partridge that gathers a brood which she did not hatch and sits on eggs which she has not laid, so is he who gets riches by unjust means and not by right. He will leave them, or they will leave him, in the midst of his days, and at his end he will be a fool."* (Jeremiah 17:11 AMP.) The reason the acquiring of the funds was unjust was because at my core I didn't believe I deserved it and the money was replacing relationships. I purged all year long and spent all my personal and business money after paying bills for the business and home. Due to the fact that I paid the bills, I wasn't aware that I was functioning in this manner as I spent every nickel and dime as I waited and anticipated the next tax season.

Has the pattern become apparent? Have you recognized the behavior as being the same as my bulimic "food" behavior? The acceptance, rejection and shame were playing out all the while I didn't have a clue, or I was not paying attention to what I was supposed to pay attention to.

Bulimia, addiction, shame, the lies pierced the very core of the business adding toxicity into it and the finances. The reality was this, I was doing only what I knew to do and nothing appeared out of the ordinary until the third year in business, which was the beginning of my awareness on how I was truly managing business. It was unhealthy, but I wasn't able to connect the dots and retrace my steps to see bulimia was running the show.

I was determined to excel far above what I had in past years. My determination became compulsion and obsession as I was driven by my need for guidance, affirmation, attention and discipline. The bulimic behavior is what came to the surface, but the core issues were unmet love needs that David and Beverly Sedlacek, explained eloquently in their book, *Cleansing the Sanctuary of the Heart: Tools for Emotional Healing*. Parents are designed to stand in the place of God for children to show up and represent the love of God, but in households where addictions are present, these love needs are not met due to one or both parents being emotionally unavailable because of his or her own addiction and therefore unable to meet the love needs of the child or children. The core love needs explained in their book are:

1. **Affection** -The responsibility of the parent to give plenty of safe, nurturing affection in the form of warm, gentle touching, hugs and kisses. This develops basis for trust, and foundation for character development.

2. **Affirmation**- To build a child's sense of worth and capability. A child's sense of both personal and corporate value flows from an adequate number of positive affirmation. Without it, the child develops a deep core of shame about his or her person. Acknowledging their strengths lets them know that they can believe in themselves. This is a place I struggled as a child, not receiving affirmation; I have to be very intentional, as a parent, about giving affirmation.

3. **Attention**- Life can get so busy that we can fail to spend the adequate quality and quantity time with children, but we must invest in them. Children thrive when they experience parents participating in their life. With adequate time and attention children receive a sense that they are important and belong in the family.

4. **Protection** - Isn't just about locks on doors and instructions. It is the development and enforcement

of family rules designed to give order to the functioning of the family. Without it, children believe they must take care of themselves. Protection says that life is under control and that they are in control of their world. Emotional protection is also important, children need to know their parents won't minimize or discount their feeling, reality nor will they allow others to do so.

5. **Discipline** - Children test boundaries. Boundaries help us establish the balance of justice and mercy. Discipline is to teach and ultimately show the child how to live as an adult. Without proper discipline a child learns to be manipulative. The Bible says this in Hebrews regarding discipline, *"And have you [completely] forgotten the divine word of appeal and encouragement in which you are reasoned with and addressed as sons? My son, do not think lightly or scorn to submit to the correction and discipline of the Lord, nor lose courage and give up and faint when you are reproved or corrected by Him; For the Lord corrects and disciplines everyone whom He loves, and He punishes, even scourges, every son whom He accepts and welcomes to His heart and cherishes."* (Hebrews 12:5-6 AMP)

6. **Comfort-** When a child experiences hurt or pain, either by scratch on the knee or bumping of the head, he or she may cry, but if the, "Don't Feel

Rule," is in place, the child may be told don't cry, and walks away without comfort by the parents. God is comfort. *"COMFORT, COMFORT My people, says your God."* (Isaiah 40:1 AMP)

While at a family member's house, my daughter aged 13, noticed the dad of her nine- year- old cousin, say to his son, "Stop that crying, you are too old to cry." She then said to me, "They will wonder later why he won't tell them anything, because he's not able to feel and express himself, get comfort and understanding." Without comfort a child blocks, numbs, medicates, or projects his/her feelings, and shows a lack of compassion, therefore forgiveness is difficult for him/her to process.

7. **Guidance**- During the journey from adolescence into adulthood, guidance is pivotal in the development of the child. *"Teach me, and I will hold my peace; and cause me to understand wherein I have erred."* (Job 6:24 AMP.) This helps the child develop a sense of direction and respect for their elders. Without guidance, children have difficulty understanding cause and effect, and decision-making is not easy for them. While in the car with my daughter, she explained to me an issue she had at school with a teacher and she raised her voice

and rolled her neck as she explained the situation to me. I listened until she finished.

I asked, "Did you say what you said to her just like that?"

She stated "No, mom, I just said it like that with you become you allow me to express how I truly feel, without judgment or not try to shut me down."

I shared with her the places she could have made some adjustments and she listened. This was a major issue with the both of us. Due to my mother being busy working to provide as a single parent and my dad physically and emotionally unavailable due to addiction I was left without guidance in all aspects. In addition to the above, I lacked financial guidance of any kind.

I began the business with some standards as to whom I would and wouldn't hire, but due to an appetite for more and a need to try to meet unmet love needs through the acquiring of money, I lost sight of all those standards. Did I really have standards or a boundary in the beginning was the question? Truly lost in the addiction, I was blinded and couldn't see because bulimia was playing out in a totally different way than I was acquainted with.

2012 tax season, our third year in business, was the climax. I decided to hire more staff; those that would go out and obtain clients, because the more clients we had, the more money we made. Being that the majority of the staff would be commissioned, I hired eight employees. As I micro- managed them because my personal life was chaotic, I became greatly overwhelmed. I was totally new to this as I went from having zero employees the first year to having eight the third year in business. All of whom did not have formal interviews, or should I say, didn't go through the process to obtain their position, but were hired because they knew me in some way. This was one of the biggest mistakes I ever made!

THE MISUNDERSTANDING OF MONEY IS THE ROOT OF ALL EVIL

I was headed home one evening after a busy and tumultuous day. I picked up the phone and dialed my sister's number. I was having so many problems with the staff at the office. I briefly explained to her the issues I was facing. One person was being deceitful, taking client's information home and preparing their tax returns. Another was preparing taxes through the store bought software, when policy advised against that. All of this went on and I overlooked it because we were still making money. Business was good, or so I thought. I erupted into tears; "I don't know what to do," I broke down on the phone in the middle of our conversation. "Fire them! How is this your business and they are doing everything you advised them not to do? Do I need to come up there?" My sister furiously questioned me. "No, I'll deal with it." I timidly replied.

Even though I had a business and appeared to have things together on the exterior, my self-worth was diminished. Though I could purchase a $600-$2500 handbag or shoes, inside I was dying, and nothing, no amount of money was enough because I was empty and money was my new "food" to feed the bulimic appetite.

The season began to come to a close, I didn't have the courage to fire anyone so I began to slowly remove the employees from the schedule giving them very few hours in hopes that they would get the picture instead of addressing the issue. That year the business grossed over $190,000 from January to March, but there was no separation between the business and myself. I began to feel prideful and ashamed at the same time. *"Pride goes before destruction, and a haughty spirit before a fall."* (Proverbs 16:18 AMP) Although I worked for everything I had, the lie speaking from within continuously told me, "I'm not worth it and I do not deserve to be in business or anything else to be exact."

I began to realize something was internally out of balance. I sought a counselor, not sure what my issues were, but I knew something had to change. The Internet is great, but can be detrimental as well because I diagnosed myself with adult Attention Deficit Disorder. I couldn't focus or pay attention, I was scatter brained. Addiction, bulimia, and shame were silently running its course in my life, but doing so very subtle. After seeing the counselor, I began to make some adjustments to my life to help me focus and concentrate. I didn't have Adult ADD, but there were issues, unmet love needs for sure.

OUT OF BALANCE, MY FIRST COUNSELING VISIT

While I waited in the lobby of the counselor's office, I felt a rush of shame take over me. I felt shame, in my head; everyone there was thinking something negative about me. The receptionist called my name, I went back to meet with the counselor. She's a petite woman, with a blonde bob. I sat on the couch as she sits on the chair across from me. She had her ink pen and notepad in her and hand and immediately asked me questions.

"What brought you here?" She was ready to write my answer on her small notepad.

"I'm not able to focus, my thoughts are all over the place, and nothing is coming together." I responded confidently.

She said, "Do you have a television in your room? If so, remove it."

I had a television in my room at the time. She then suggested that I not read anything mind stimulating before I went to bed. The counselor suggested I keep a journal on my nightstand to jot down ideas or thoughts to clear my mind. I was desperate and willing to do almost anything for the internal madness and chaos to stop.

As I sat on the couch, I began to tell her about my childhood, which included molestation and the one incident where my mom beat me while the molester restrained me. Tears began to well in my eyes and I began to cry. I told the story and I felt sad. I told myself I had processed it and was okay, but the reality was I had just begun my journey to retrace my steps to the past.

My counseling visits were short lived that year because I thought I had it all figured out after that one session. Man, was I wrong. I had so much more I needed to process and feel. I continued with the bulimic cycle and purged all the money I had earned. By December 31st, I was broke all over again, nothing saved, nothing planned, just anticipating the purge for the next tax season.

KNOWING WHEN TO FOLD

Things went downhill from there. I desperately wanted to do something different. A few of my employees returned from year three including the receptionist, who was awesome by the way, and the office manager. My sister came on board as the watchman on the wall, to keep me aware of how I was moving around. That wasn't her official title, but that's what she did for me, she was a manager and because of her, I began to make necessary changes in the business. She was truly sent from God to help me see how I was doing in business. All new employees were interviewed and completed an employment application. This time they all went through the process without skipping any steps. The staff really enjoyed having my sister there. My sister, who happened to be the office manager, was the only person who saw how I was moving around and had the courage to tell me what I was doing wasn't in alignment with the labor standards. I am truly grateful for her presence in the business she held me accountable and that's what I needed, but never knew how to ask for it.

Due to the business only operating seasonally, the staff left once it was over. I needed more money to feed the bulimic behavior. The more money I had, the more I felt worthy, protected, and ashamed. I made adjustments to keep more for myself by lowering my office manager pay, even though she was with me from the beginning of time. I had her and another staff member bite the bullet and take the pay cut instead of me. The office manager left because of this and the business suffered after her departure. She brought many clients, but they followed her when she left. I was devastated and disgrace consumed me. The sinful nature blamed her for the business misfortune because I was unwilling to see my own behavior.

I was in shock when my office manager left, but I needed someone who had experience in the office. I reached out to a temp service for accounting and tax professionals and was sent a woman who had something I needed. Sandra had a great deal of knowledge in bookkeeping. She wanted to expand her knowledge in tax preparation and I had a wealth of knowledge in that. She was awesome. I didn't realize it, but she was sent to help me get the business financial plan together. I missed it and can only reflect as to how I could have done things differently. Shame about the chaotic business and financial savvy kept me from allowing anyone in that area, although I needed help. I let her go even though she did nothing wrong, but I didn't have the courage to tell her. I called the temp service and they told her without any notice from me. The office manager/sister advised me to tell her, but I couldn't because I was too ashamed.

A few days later, Sherita, my office manager/sister, came to me with concerns about her pay. The business paid her a weekly salary for working at least 35 hours a week. She was on salary, her salary should be consistent no matter what, but due to personal financial bulimic addiction, I was only concerned with how much I made as the owner.

She stated, "You know you can't change your employee's wages or salary when you feel like it? That's not the proper way to do it according to the law and guidelines."

In shame, pride, and arrogance, I went on to say, "I can if I want to,"

"You can, but not with me because I'm not going to allow you to." She snapped back.

I humbled myself and listened to her, and then I made the proper adjustments for the betterment of my business and myself. After that day, I implemented several changes as to the type of client we would serve and how we would be accountable for their returns. Due to the changes we implemented, I lost business, but was willing to lose anything to gain peace and sanity. We went from grossing $190,000 to $53,000, this drop affected my self-worth and I began to feel humiliated because I was losing what I thought validated my worth. I thought to myself, I'm trying to make changes for the better and I'm losing money, and there were others who were not changing and their business was at a steady increase. I even questioned God. "Lord I'm making changes to better myself and my business and I have taken a loss, it doesn't seem fair." Nevertheless, I contemplated and made the necessary changes even though they hurt.

I thought downsizing and bringing in diversity was the solution to my problem, but I was wayyyyy off, enjoying the binge, the guilt, and shame that came immediately afterwards, I looked forward to the purge. Which one was the lesser of the two evils? I'm not sure, but one thing I knew was they both gave me feelings of completeness, acceptance, and worthiness. Those watching me from the outside thought I had it together, but if someone came a little closer, he or she would have discovered there were indeed skeletons in my closet. My tax bill was unpaid about $9000.00 and I lived on section 8 public housing and received food stamps. I was even afraid to move to a house that required me paying all of the rent or mortgage because I had a fear of not having enough money to pay rent and I self-sabotaged everything.

Because I wasn't truly ready to accept my reality that the business was taking a downward turn, I went and made another poor decision. I decided to open a second location, thinking this would help the business as well. We did make a turn for the better, but there was no planning, no thought process, it was based upon pure emotion.

A man or woman ruled by his/her feelings is not wise. There was no wisdom or thought that went into opening another location it was all emotion. I needed to appear as if I had things together so I taught tax preparation classes to get more qualified employees and it worked. I did more marketing, a commercial, made flyers and door hangers; I thought all this would work to get me back on track, too. To my dismay, none of it helped with financial growth in the business.

After experiencing a decrease in business profit and having a taste of peace, I was still unaware of the financial bulimic behavior, and once again like the years before, by December 31st, I was broke all over again. Shame was the cause of my problems, there was a deep sense of inadequacy and it seeped into the business like raw sewage.

EDGE OF CHAOS

All the staff I taught in the latter part of 2013 became employees, and I wanted to right my wrong regarding wages. This idea allowed me to pay the employees their worth even if I had to take a loss. The second location was up and ready and the commercial was on the television. This season was different, because I had no planning, things went badly, and my flaws began to show with my employees. They began to work in January of 2014, and in past years they would receive their first check by the 3rd week in the month, but this year I had no money and the Internal Revenue Service did something new with releasing funds. Normally we would prepare the client's return, submit it to the federal and state agency and when the client's funds are released by the agency, through a third party bank, our fee would be collected. This would happen by the third week in January and the business would have funds to cover payroll, but not this year. We didn't receive funds until February and my employees worked almost a month without pay. To top that off, when they received their first check, they only received a portion of their pay. I was ashamed because I was being exposed; my flaws were coming into the light. I needed to look good on the outside no matter what was going on with me and my worth was attached to how others perceived me. I told myself if they saw me as I was, broken, they wouldn't like me, but time was revealing my hidden and secret thing.

"For the time is coming when everything that is covered will be revealed, and all that is secret will be made known to all." (Matthew 10:26 NLT). My time had come and I

couldn't hide or run from my truth any longer. I was finally exposed and it devastated me. The feeling I had about being found out about bulimia was the same feeling and emotions I had when I was exposed about the business and finance bulimia.

There were several people I taught in 2013 and they came through various ways, but one was sent just for me. God was again trying to rescue me from myself. We received a résumé in the mail, and honestly I was baffled that she sent it to the business. Later, I realized she was sent from God. She had a bookkeeping background and wanted to learn the tax side of accounting. Before she completed the courses I asked her to join our team and she accepted. I was truly grateful for her, but l didn't initially utilize her in her expertise because I wanted her to do something else. She was what I needed, but didn't have the ability to articulate it.

She was my heart's desire and God knew that He sent what I needed. She was eager to learn tax information even though she specialized in bookkeeping. In March of that same year, I realized her true purpose for the business, and me, which was what came natural to her, bookkeeping. Shame and fear of being seen kept me from allowing someone in, to see my true issue and help me get things cleaned up. It was something different about this employee, I felt relaxed and I stopped suffering in silence and allowed her to be great in the area of her greatness. Wow, was she great! We had to go backwards some years in the bookkeeping to get me caught up to where I should have been. She completed the accounting and bookkeeping for previous and current years, created a business budget, profit and loss statements, balance sheets, which I took and used to get a $15,000 loan, employee schedule, and forecasting for the following year, according to the numbers from the current year. She was a breath of fresh air.

There were days I was in awe at the value she brought to my life and business. I would literally be in tears because of my gratitude for her ability to know exactly what I needed. All the things I needed to have in place for the foundation of the business to be repaired she brought. Before she began it was clearly established that she would leave in May of 2014, because she would move back up north. I wasn't ready for her to leave, I needed more guidance, I felt abandoned when she left, not realizing she could have performed the same task from afar. I needed accountability and with her gone I spiraled out of control again. Her work was for the surface issue, but my core issues were still unattended to.

That same year the business grossed $77,000 and I spent 34% of the earnings on payroll. I wanted to right the wrong as previously stated in the payment of the employees, but I wasn't able to accept my reality relating to the financial state of my business. There were two locations and it became very apparent that I had to let one of them go. I wasn't ready to let go and accept reality although I saw the direction things were headed, but I still held on.

After the season ended, I had these two locations that were just occupying space. I only worked from these locations January through April and I wasn't able to afford the rent. I had moved and wasn't on Section 8 anymore and I was afraid. I battled with God and myself. I felt as if God had forsaken me.

My thoughts and prayers went something like this:

"I have done all you asked of me, why is this happening to me? Why is the business failing? When I'm doing what I should and others are not. What did I do wrong to deserve this? Surely others are doing things they shouldn't be, why me? Why does the business you entrusted in my hands have to fail? It's not fair!"

These questions plagued me and I got an answer. The first answer was, "Why not you?" According to (Jeremiah 17:9-10, AMP), *"The heart is deceitful above all things and it is exceedingly perverse and corrupt and severely, mortally sick! Who can know it perceive, understand, because acquainted with his own heart and mind?"* The Bible says, *"I the Lord search the mind, I try the heart, even to give to every man according to his ways…….. and doings."* God was trying to heal me within and the external issues, the money, was a wall that was placed for protection, but it kept God and people from knowing me and stopped me from seeing my core issues. The fall of the business offered me an opportunity to search my heart and see the heart of the matter, which was shame, lies, and bulimic behavior.

The second answer came later as I read Jeremiah. I told God all that I was doing or performing and He said to me through (Jeremiah 11:4-5 AMP) *"Listen to My voice and do according to all that I command you. So will you be My people, and I will be your God. That I (God) may perform the oath which I (God) swore to your fathers, to give them a land flowing with milk and honey."* I realized I had been *performing* for God, with all that I had been doing. However, He was more interested in me being than doing, so He could do exactly what He said.

THE TRANSITION

Closing the business in the fall of 2014 was hard. I felt as if a part of me was dying. I grieved the loss of this location, like someone would grieve the loss of a family member. This business was first a thought/idea then eventually it came to life and I labored to nurture it so it would grow. I saw it grow every year. When it was at its third year, I witnessed it slowly move until it was on life support. There were choices I had to let go of or spend a great deal of money, time and effort, repairing so, I had to count the cost to see if it was worth it. I let go, and letting go was one of the most difficult, but most beautiful things I've done. I cried many nights because I believed my worth was so entangled in the success or failure of the business. I was enmeshed in it and the success or failure of it, felt as if it was a reflection of me. What was going on with the business was what I was experiencing internally. I was in transition as well as the thing connected to me

The sun shone very brightly on that moving day. I had a friend of mine from the church assisting me with moving the office furniture and equipment. As I walked into the office, I felt physically able to do this, but emotionally and mentally I was unprepared. There were feelings and attachments to the stuff I had in the office and it meant a lot to me. I began to pack the boxes with the desk items and small things that had to be removed before the large items could be removed. As I went through each and every item I was saddened. The reality of closing began to settle within. I thought to myself, "The toil and labor from my first business was all in vain," and it was so unbelievable. Johnny, my friend, who helped me move, was eager to get the furniture out of the building. He came in and hurriedly started packing and boxing things right away before he sat them outside. I immediately became livid, in my mind he was not handling my things in the manner that I thought he should, but really I was angry because I was emotionally attached to everything that was in the office. This is why I wasn't good in relationships because items became more valuable than people. From the filing cabinet, to the gem clip, to the desk calendar, I was committed to everything. I could think back to when it was first purchased and found its way into my office space. Each and every item in that office meant something to me and I seriously needed time to process my feelings as I examined all of the supplies, chairs and staplers, before they were put into the truck. When he began to place the things outside without allowing me to look at it, it was as if he was attacking me and I didn't like it.

I finally became angry and lashed out, "Don't throw my things outside like that; I need to look at them and give you permission to move them outside!" Johnny had a confused look on his face as if he couldn't understand my fervor responded about moving items. "I came here to move this furniture and that's what I'm doing, it may not be moved how you want it moved, but I'm moving it out because when the truck arrives it will be outside already!" He snapped back.

We were both able to understand one another in that very moment. We sat down and I began to express my heart issues to him. I told him how emotionally connected I was to the furniture and how I needed this process to view and examine everything because it was a part of me. I was really emotionally connected to the idea or the story that I was telling myself about the business. After our conversation, we continued packing and I finished the rest at my own pace. The day was long and emotional. This all seemed so final. It was a piece of my life for many years, five to be exact. The truck finally pulled up to the storefront with another gentleman who helped to move the equipment and furniture. I was so glad he came later in the day after my breakdown because I had time to process my feelings. We moved forward and took the equipment to the storage without any emotional outbursts from me. This was considered progress.

As I mentioned before, I borrowed $15,000 and used it towards my business. I utilized all of the business furniture as collateral to get the loan. I had no plan for the money, but the money validated my worth, I felt worthy again even though I knew the business location would be closing down. I needed to feel validation and worthiness and the money was my armor. I paid my debtors and purged the remainder of the funds.

I had a different situation going on by the end of this particular tax season. Both locations closed and I was working and commuting to Montgomery, AL to work for a non-profit organization, and I was petrified. I was not accustomed to working for someone, given a time to be at work and being paid on a monthly basis, this was all new to me and scary as well.

I loved what I did as an entrepreneur and I couldn't see or imagine not being one. Shame began to sink in, in an all too familiar tune and tell me a story which went a little something like this: your clients aren't going to let you do their taxes, you lost your respect or credibility when you closed the offices, no one wants to go to a preparer who doesn't have a location, and you will lose all those clients. Life was uncertain and I didn't like it, I felt powerless, I needed to know, not knowing was scary for me. Being in control was a structure I created to protect myself as a child because the molestation, the violations to my body, I had no control over. Therefore I made an unconscious vow to be in control and never allow any harm to happen to me. Amongst this structure were many more that I struggled with. Below is a list of what we may struggle with taken from David and Beverly Sedlacek, *Cleansing the Sanctuary of the*

Heart: Tools for Emotional Healing. A Companion Workbook for Personal or Group Use. 2011.

Shame core- Lies we believe about ourselves, others, and God.

Control/controlling- Fear that life will be totally out of control if I am not in charge.

Self-dependence- Lack of trust in other and God.

Negativity-Hopelessness

Self-righteousness- low self-worth, pride, unable to make mistakes.

Judgementalism- Lack of trust that God will righteously judge.

Victim/Victimizer- Bitterness, lack of trust, bad things are always happening to you.

Caretaking- Lack of trust in others and God.

Family Roles-martyr, hero- Lack of understanding of who we are; pride.

Perfectionism- Lie that if I'm not perfect, I am not good at all.

Self-sabotage- Lie that I deserved to fail and do not deserve to succeed.

Performance Orientation- Lie that I must perform to be acceptable to God and others.

Fears- rejection, abandonment - Lie that I will be rejected or abandoned if I offended someone.

Codependency- My sense of personal identity is interwoven with that of another person.

Addictions- Comfort sought in anything or anyone other than God.

Conflict Avoidance- Moving away from address situation that may not seem favorable.

This list revealed several of these structures that were in place in my life that surfaced in my childhood. When I, or anyone, operates from these structures, we are moving as frightened little boys or girls. We must all experience or go through a death to self, which strips us from holding onto these structures. According to Galatians 2:20 NLT, it says, *"My old self has been crucified with Christ. It is no longer I who live, but Christ lives in me. So I live in this earthly body by trusting in the Son of God, who loved me and gave himself for me."* (Colossians 3:3 NLT) reiterates, *"For you died to this life, and your real life is hidden with Christ in God."* Only God can create new experiences or set up to overwrite the one we have to tear down these structures and set our life on a new trajectory.

LIVING INSIDE OUT ON PURPOSE

I'm a huge fan of movies and the movie, *Inside Out*, is a great example of the setup or experience we need to change our trajectory and heal our wounds. Riley is an 11-year-old girl who moved from Minnesota to San Francisco right before her 12th birthday because her dad received a new job. Twelve is a very pivotal age in exploring and learning who we are. Jesus, at the age of twelve, stayed at the temple after traveling to Jerusalem with His parents without their permission as He began to explore and learn more of who He was, (Luke 2:41-51). Riley hated that she had to move because all she knew and all her core memories, which were ninety percent joyful, were created in her old hometown. Her core memories powered her island of personality. Riley had to move from her old school in Minnesota. She didn't see any good in her move to this new place she felt as if this was the worst thing that happened to her. Her emotions, Joy, was running her life and worked effortlessly to keep her from experiencing anything other than Joy, but Riley had another emotion she needed to experience, sadness. Sadness didn't see a purpose for herself as an emotion, because Joy was determined to keep Riley from experiencing Sadness. All of Riley's memories from her old town were one way; there were no mixed emotions within her days, only one single emotion. If she started the day off sad, her day was remembered as being sad, if it was joyful, it was remembered as joyful, if anger dominated, that's how she remembered the day.

She had a difficult time making connections and began to feel a new emotion, sadness as she cried in front of her new friends. Riley purposed in her heart to go back to where all the joyful moments happened in her life, her old hometown. She purchased a bus ticket and ran away from home to get back to her old town. Through this process Riley's emotions, joy and sadness became lost, and she was only able to experience, fear, anger, and disgust, while Joy, and Sadness, worked effortlessly to get back to headquarters. While they were lost, Riley was slowly losing her island of personality, which housed her core memories and fueled her personality. As she sat on the bus she recalled a time when she played hockey; she originally remembered this moment to be totally joyful, but she recalled a moment of sadness within that memory this time.

Running away was the experience that gave Riley a new trajectory and allowed her to live life to the fullest. She sat on the bus and remembered her hockey game where she missed a shot causing her team to lose the game. She initially only remembered the experience as being totally joyful, but she replayed it again noticing sadness was present, and because of sadness, Riley's family and friends comforted her which changed Riley's mood to joy. Riley was now in control of her emotions because she found sadness, which was pivotal in her process to experiencing true joy. She exited the bus before it left the station and returned home. While in the headquarters, her brain, the emotions looked to Joy to save the day as Riley returned home to her parents, but Joy gave room for Sadness to play her role in her life. After she arrived home, Riley's parents greeted her at the door and she wept as her parents comforted and hugged her while she explained what was going on within. This experience created a new core memory with sadness and joy in one memory, which led to the redemption of Riley. This experience set Riley on a new course of being able to experience life as more than black and white; she could now embrace life as it came and be healed through the process.

Like Riley's story, God gives us experiences to tear down those walls, which shape our character that we may experience a death to our old self and live in freedom.

EMBRACING BROKENNESS

My sixth year in business I learned my yearly brokenness was an outer expression of my inward self. I found myself broke with money and broken without money; therefore I came to a place of acceptance of my brokenness to truly be made whole. In (Jeremiah 1:10 AMP), God said, *"See, I have this day appointed you to the oversight of the nations and of the kingdoms to root out and pull down, to destroy and to overthrow, to build and to plant."*

I understand from this text and from, *Inside Out*, before I could be whole, I had to go through this process of accepting my brokenness. God had to get to the root cause of many issues in my life, pull down structures I lived with to protect myself, and destroy and overthrow the lies I believed that caused me to function in bulimic, shame based behavior. This year was the total demolition of my island of character that causes me to victimize myself and seek comfort through bingeing and purging. Closing the business was a painful experience. For ten years I used binging and purging in different forms as a coping skill, and through the business, I was still using those same mechanisms.

I worked from a friend's office this season, no employees to manage, just my behavior, which had gotten me into this predicament and me. I hadn't truly embraced where I was, even though in 2014 the bookkeeper and I created a budget for me to utilize. It was later revealed that the budget wasn't the real issue. I could have had 10 budgets and ended right where I started because the binging and purging was connected to unmet love needs. Until I faced the pain of my unmet love needs the issue, bulimic behavior, would continue to manifest.

The year began differently, I had a job and was able to pay my current bills and debt I incurred, but I hadn't embraced the slow and steady pace of receiving funds. I was trained and accustomed to "binge, or gather my funds," and this new way that God was trying to teach me was scary even to the thought. I had a battle going on within me. I didn't want to let go my idea of the business in order to get something else, peace. I left the job because going back to what I knew was comfortable. I wasn't sure how to balance both so one had to go. The season, even though it was planned from a budgeting perspective didn't go that way, I lost clients through the move and I still didn't have enough, so I believed. I grossed $42,000 this season, there were no employees and bookkeeper so all the planning went out of the window.

I paid off all of my credit cards because I didn't want to worry about paying them throughout the year. I thought I was doing something totally different from the previous years, but in reality, I was doing the same thing. I lived in Pike Road, Alabama, which is one hour and thirty minutes from Birmingham where I worked. This new place was different and unfamiliar to me and I had a hard time accepting my reality. My daughter was home schooled at the time and I stayed in Birmingham with family the majority of the time during the season. After the season was over I came home to Pike Road and continued to purge financially. Once again the financial bulimic behavior was in control and by August of this year, I was broke and needed money to pay rent. I borrowed $5000.00 from a friend, I was hitting my bottom and totally unaware of how I got there. In October, I was reminded I paid all my credit cards off so I phoned those that I didn't close to send me a new card. I again charged over $8000.00 in debt on my credit cards before December, I was broke again and unable to pay my rent or even buy food for my house. I sent several résumés out and applied to several jobs, but was unsuccessful in finding one.

In December, my sister and I hosted an event, "Encounter Women's Experience," and one of the facilitators I mentioned in the earlier chapters, JoAnne Palmer, came and presented The Cycle of Dysfunction from the book, *Cleansing the Sanctuary of the Heart*. I had heard this cycle of dysfunction many times and knew it from a firsthand perspective. Unbeknownst to me, I was at another place in my journey, but still in this cycle of dysfunction. I would have loved to believe I was doing something different or a new creator as, (2 Corinthians 5:17 NIV), stated, "*Therefore, if anyone is in Christ, the new creation has come: The old has gone, the new is here!"* However, I was in my journey for newness, because newness in Christ is not an instant process, salvation is the work of a lifetime.

At the conclusion of Encounter Women's Experience, it was clear to me that my behavior with bulimia and food was the same in my business and finances and at the core was an unmet love need. These unmet needs were my true issues: lack of comfort, guidance, discipline, and protection. Money was not my issue, it was what came to the surface, like food. Albert Einstein said, *"The solution is never at the level of the problem,"* and I understand and found this to be true. I reviewed my bank statements and noticed in one month I deposited $7,000.00 into my personal account and spent $7,000.00. My bills didn't total this amount, neither did I gamble or seriously shopped. I was caught in the cycle and God was creating a way out. According to (1 Corinthians 10:13 AMP) *"For no temptation (no trial regarded as enticing to sin), [no matter how it comes or where it leads] has overtaken you and laid hold on you that is not common to man [that is, no temptation or trial has come to you that is beyond human resistance and that is not adjusted and adapted and belonging to human experience, and such as man can bear]. But God is faithful [to His Word and to His compassionate nature], and He [can be trusted] not to let you be tempted and tried and assayed beyond your ability and strength of resistance and power to endure, but with the temptation He will [always] also provide the way out (the means of escape to a landing place), that you may be capable and strong and powerful to bear up under it patiently."* I wanted to break this cycle, but fear of what life would be like not functioning in this manner was just as scary to me, as explained by Paul in (Romans 7:15, 19-20 AMP), *"For I do not understand my own actions [I am baffled, bewildered]. I do not practice or accomplish what I wish, but I do the very thing that I loathe [which my moral instinct condemns]. For I fail to practice the good deeds I desire to do, but the evil deeds that I do not desire to do are what I am [ever] doing. Now if I do what I do not desire to do, it is no longer I doing it [it is not myself that acts], but the sin [principle] which dwells within me [fixed and operating in my soul]."* The sin principle was truly dwelling in me because I honestly wanted to do something different, and I was looking for that way of escape or for God's setup to put me on a new trajectory.

I had a conversation with a client and we were going back to previous years to prepare his tax returns from 2007-2012. We began the process with 2007 and worked our way up to 2012. He calculated several business expenses for 2007 and was 85% complete with 2008. 2008 was a difficult year for him because there were so many expenses and going back through the information caused him to revisit what was going on in his life at the time. He came into my office one day and we began to talk.

"How do you feel? You're almost finished with the most difficult year of 2008." I inquired.

"I'm anxious and excited because I've lived with these skeletons for so long. Not having it is just as scary as having it." He replied, as he looked me square in the eyes.

The reality was, he wasn't certain of the unknown. He knew where he stood with the issues, but because it abided within him, he didn't know life without it. This was my same feeling, for years I lived in a bulimic cycle and shame hijacked my prefrontal cortex, and the way of escape appeared to be painful because it was unfamiliar. One of my structures was control, which came from a lack of protection, which came from the molestation and not feeling protected from my victimizer. As a way of escape, I would have to give up my ability to be in control and trust God with all of me. As a child I wasn't able to trust my parents with me, so how would I know what it looked like to trust God with protecting me? The only way out was to go through the process of allowing myself to not be in control, no matter how scary it may have appeared to be. In another excerpt from *Anatomy of the Soul*, Curt Thompson brilliantly described the brain as it relates to sin and redemption. In our childhood, paths are created or laid down that have us responding to situations in the same way. He coined the phrase, *"Neurons that wire together, fire together,"* meaning when we are faced with situations in life that gives us the same emotional feeling as the first path that was laid down, we will respond the same way. The way out or off this path is through the way of escape or a new trajectory. God was creating a way of escape for me, the setup to put me on a new trajectory when it came to my feeling of rejection, being misguided, and control. He was setting up a way of escape for me, although I wasn't aware. The way of escape was scary, but it was healthy, and I knew in my head it was better, but my heart battled with the idea of operating differently as it relates to the business and finances in another way.

My Truth!

What does it look like, is it packaged with a pretty bow?

Does it sound like a beautiful symphony?

Does it smell like fresh cut roses on a summer day? My truth, oh wait, you'll see!
My truth!

It looks like hurts and pain, like a cut within and the blood can't drain.

It sounds like a collision of two screeching freight trains.

It smells like a fresh catch of fish in the middle of the sea.

My truth no matter how unappealing it may appear to be.

My truth I embrace because it has help evolve me.

My truth can and will be healed! I must first accept my truth is real!

Chapter 6
You Spot It, You Got It.

"As in water face answers to and reflects face, so the heart of man to man."(Proverbs 27:19 AMP)

During the darkest places in the controversy with bulimia, there was only one person who saw me. She was a close family friend. She asked my sister if I was bulimic, but my sister didn't know at the time, so she said no. Later on my sister asked me about it, and I stated I wasn't and questioned the woman's intention behind the question to deflect and change the conversation. The idea that someone saw me brought more anxiety within than actual binging and purging. Although my behavior was a cry to be seen and heard, being seen was very unsettling within. "If you spot it, you got it," is a concept from the book, *Cleansing the Sanctuary of the Heart,* by David and Beverly Sedlacek. I wasn't quite sure what it meant upon reading about it, but while at a retreat it became clear. When I am able to see someone else, they became a reflection of me. Later God revealed that he wanted me to see myself in those whom I could see so clearly.

Years passed and I had a conversation with our family friend. I told her what I learned about the aforementioned concept from the book. I then followed it with the verse: (Proverbs 27:19 AMP) *"As in water face answers to and reflects face, so the heart of man to man."* If one looks into water, pond, pool or lake he or she would see his own reflection like a mirror, therefore his face is answering his face. So, the heart of man-to-man, means what I see in others is a reflection of what's in me. This may be a hard pill to swallow, well it was for me. I didn't believe that this was true. I could remember how many times I was able to spot or see things in others, but my own issues somehow eluded me.

After explaining this concept to her and sharing a story she stated she wasn't bulimic. Though that was true in the aspects of food, I believed and lived through bulimia manifesting in other areas of my life. I experienced bulimia showing up in finances, excessive exercise, fasting, and in my relationships. The root of the bulimia was a lie, shame, and distorted view of reality, rejection issues and a need for control. Although she wasn't able to identify with the surface part of bulimia that we all know, it didn't mean she hadn't spotted herself in me. She saw me during my bulimia behavior with food, and I saw her in that present moment, only because I saw myself first. There is still more to be revealed behind her seeing me, but in time all things will be revealed.

I had another experience with someone from a church I attended. I didn't like how this person moved around. The person was controlling and domineering, in my opinion. I truly despised what I saw in the person. I couldn't even be around this individual because it made my blood boil. It wasn't until I began to see, process and understand my control issues that I was able to deal with the person differently. When I became aware of my issues and stopped focusing on this individual's issue, I was able to interact with her differently.

One day she came to me and stated, "I didn't know you had rejection issues." I stated confidently, "I don't have rejection issues," and she in turn stated, "It seems like you have them." I didn't respond, I felt something I didn't like, so I politely walked away. Time went by and I had the same feeling I had when other people mentioned the word rejection. I went to a retreat in January 2015 and discovered that I, in fact, had rejection issues that were unbeknownst to me; she spotted me regarding this issue. If this saying is correct, and Biblically we have found that to be true, then the person, too, dealt with rejection.

The Biblical character, David, is a good person to help explain this concept a little further. For years David was loyal to King Saul, but that didn't stop Saul from trying to kill David. David could clearly see that Saul was a murderer but he missed it in himself. In (2 Samuel Chapter 11), David took one of his most loyal soldiers wife, Uriah's wife, and slept with her while Uriah was away at battle. When it was discovered she was pregnant, David tried to cover his tracks and sent for Uriah so he could lay with his wife. Uriah, because of his commitment and loyalty to the King, would not lay with his wife, after several attempts to do so. David sent Uriah with his own death letter back to battle and placed him on the front line to be killed, David was a murderer just like Saul.

When we are not able to see ourselves, God brings others into our lives to help us see ourselves. In (2 Samuel 12:1-7, AMP), God sent Nathan to hold a mirror to David's face so he could see himself clearly. *"AND THE Lord sent Nathan to David. He came and said to him, "There were two men in a city, one rich and the other poor. The rich man had very many flocks and herds, but the poor man had nothing but one little ewe lamb, which he had bought and brought up, and it grew up with him and his children. It ate of his own morsel, drank from his own cup, lay in his bosom, and was like a daughter to him. Now a traveler came to the rich man, and to avoid taking one of his own flock or herd to prepare for the wayfaring man who had come to him, he took the poor man's lamb and prepared it for his guest. Then David's anger was greatly kindled against the man, and he said to Nathan, As the Lord lives, the man who has done this is a son [worthy] of death.*

He shall restore the lamb fourfold, because he did this thing and had no pity. Then Nathan said to David, You are the man! Thus says the Lord, the God of Israel I anointed you king of Israel, and I delivered you out of the hand of Saul."

David was able to clearly spot the heart issue of the man in the story and he made a judgment about what should happen to the "rich man" due to his actions. After spotting it, Nathan the prophet in verse 7 tells David that he is the "rich man" in the story. Later we are able to see how spotting such thing made changes in his life. (Psalms 51) is the byproduct, lament of David after he realized he too was a murderer and no different from Saul. David had a godly sorrow that hurt him deeply when he realized the person he judged, he too, was that person.

I don't suggest the idea of "spotting" someone is always for the person who's doing the spotting. The seeing could very well be for the other party. After "spotting" or "seeing" self and becoming aware of our strongholds, we are able to "spot," "see," others to assist them along their journey. Sharing stories helps others understand that I, too, struggle with or have struggled with and what I may currently see in them. Stories are very powerful tools in spotting or seeing someone, because it gives the other person an opportunity to "see" or "spot" himself or herself in someone else's story. In the story with David and Nathan, Nathan shared a story and David judged it then Nathan stated David was the person he judged in the story.

JUDGE NOT

My daughter had truly been my heart answers to heart person that I see clearly. I can remember when she was five years old, I was 25 years old at the time, and I was caught up in the bulimic cycle. I wasn't focused in any area of my life, not even on my own child. I was employed as a shampoo assistant at a local salon when this woman came in to get her hair styled. This woman was different than any other woman who frequented visited the salon. She was interesting and intriguing. I would often wash her hair and we would have great and inspirational conversations.

One day she told me to pay attention to my daughter because God speaks to me through her. I really didn't understand what she meant by those words, but I listened and tried to be more attentive to my daughter. Years later, I truly began to understand what she meant by her words as I became healthier.

I can remember learning what it means to "judge not" as in (Matthew 7:1-5 AMP), through an experience with my daughter. My three-year-old niece stayed the night over our house one night and she urinated in my daughter's bed while she slept. The next morning Jamiah scolded her because she wet her bed. This was an accident because the night before she had too much to water before bedtime. A few days later, Jamiah, who was nine at the time, urinated in my bed. This quickly reminded me of (Matthew 7:1-5 AMP), which states, *"Do not judge, criticize and condemn others, so that you may not be judged and criticized and condemned yourselves. For just as you judge and criticize and condemn others, you will be judged and criticized and condemned, and in accordance with the measure you [use to] deal out to others, it will be dealt out again to you. Why do you stare from without at the very small particle that is in your brother's eye but do not become aware of and consider the beam of timber that is in your own eye? Or how can you say to your brother, Let me get the tiny particle out of your eye, when there is the beam of timber in your own eye? You hypocrite, first get the beam of timber out of your own eye, and then you will see clearly to take the tiny particle out of your brother's eye."* My daughter now sat in the very place that she judged, criticized, and scolded my niece in.

The concept of "you spot it, you got it," also applies to children and their relationship with their parents or caregivers. As children we spot or see things in our parents or caregivers and we make judgments against them and vow to not be like them when we grow up. The reality is we only know how to be like our parents or caretakers, because that's the only example we had. Even in our quest to do something different from our parents we do the same thing, but it may look different. A vow is a pledge or personal commitment, but the vows we make as children are made from a place of judgment, resentment or bitterness towards our parents or caretakers. The outcomes of these vows are harmful to our person. *"When you make a vow to the Lord your God, you shall not be slack in paying it, for the Lord your God will surely require it of you, and slackness would be sin in you. But if you refrain from vowing, it will not be sin in you. The vow which has passed your lips you shall be watchful to perform, a voluntary offering which you have made to the Lord your God, which you have promised with your mouth."* (Deuteronomy 23:21-23 AMP). As children the vows we make are internal vows and some we spoke aloud. I'm sure you can remember being a child and saying things to yourself or even amongst siblings, like "when I get older and have children I will never," If you didn't, I did, and because the Word is true, we will perform the vow or its sin to us.

This reigns true in my life. I spotted my mother struggle with managing money, weight, and men. Though my mother always had a job and she was determined and able to make money, she struggled with managing it because she put it in the wrong places. I also judged my mom as being "money hungry" because she worked a lot to provide for her children and I vowed to not be like her in this area, but to my dismay, I became the flip side to that coin and didn't work a lot and was stagnant on being able to financially provide for myself and daughter because the way I was telling the story. My siblings and I were always dressed nice, but there were times the power would be disconnected and we didn't have the food we wanted to eat. My mother moved back and forth with her mother because of her money management issues, from my perspective. At the time, she had been in debtors' court more than twice. My mother was always on the latest diet and concerned about her weight. When a new diet came out or some new diet pills were on the market, she would be on the diet or have the pills, we could always count on her for that. She had several male friends that I saw in my childhood after divorcing my dad. I can remember being really upset with my mom when she had a male friend over because he would have her attention, and some nights I would cry myself to sleep because she had company.

The places I saw her in turmoil and struggle, I made unconscious internal vows and judgments and I struggled in the same places. I appeared to be doing well financially and it appeared that I was doing something different from my mom for a number of years. My business seemed to be growing and my finances looked as if they were in order, until I had to go to my mother, the very person I judged, and ask for money to pay my rent because my money was gone, through a binge. It wasn't because I didn't have enough; it was because I wasn't able to manage what I had, just as I judged my mother. I found myself filing bankruptcy for my business and myself due to the vow and judgment I made about her. It's clear that I struggled with weight, but the struggle was more internal than external. Unlike my mother whose issues were more visible, the bulimic behavior went unnoticed for quite some time, and it appeared that I was doing something different, but it was the same. We both had a distorted image of self that was based in shame.

When I became an adult, I slept with my door closed all the time. I remember saying I wouldn't close my door when I had company over because as a little girl I felt abandoned and shut out when my mother closed her door when her male company was over. Well that didn't stop me from repeating the same cycle. I, too, had several male friends when Jamiah was younger, and I know she was affected by my action. Her father passed when she was three years old and every friend I allowed her to meet; she thought he was her new dad. None of the relationships have worked out so far. The reality is I didn't know how to do anything differently, and my unconscious internal vows and judgments were fulfilled because the Word of God is true.

I judged my dad as being sickly, emotional unavailable, and weak because of his addiction. In my dating life, I found myself dating men that were "weak" or without coping mechanisms. It was a slow progress with the men I dated. My daughter's dad drank alcohol to cope with life, the barber I dated smoked marijuana, and the church member I dated with was on crack cocaine. When I thought I was doing better in the dating arena, I met a guy in the service, but he also had issues with alcohol and women. How did I find myself dating these types of guys? As we discovered, the Word of God is true and the internal unconscious judgments I made about my parents played out in my life. The guys I dated were parts of my dad that I judged and didn't accept, so much so that I dated the very thing I judged about him. I found myself being a caretaker to men because when my dad was shot, when we were around him, we cared for him. Through that experience I learned to relate to men as their caretakers. My dad also minimized everything in life, nothing was ever a big deal, and it was always belittled. Of course, I did the same thing because that's what I spotted in my dad and judged.

I struggled to honor my father and mother although this is the first commandment with a promise according to (Exodus 20:12 NKJV), *"Honor your father and your mother that your days may be long upon the land which the Lord your God is giving you."*

This was a lament, about my mother I wrote in my diary:

Lament April 19th 2015

Now, Lord, as I sit here in Birmingham at my mother's house I'm angry and confused, Father. This woman you gave me as a mother, why? Right now I could say some really hurtful things to her because she just said something that was really hurtful to me. I could say that I never want to see her again and I really don't like her and being around her is never a joyous moment for me. She really doesn't understand the impact that she has had on my life, and how I still to this day would like for her to be proud of me. She literally makes me sick at this moment.

But You, oh God, knew what I needed to make me who you know I would be. You gave me the "perfect" person to be my mother. Even though I may not see her as being perfect for me, God I believe you see what I need.

I write this because as I stood in my mother's room and took my clothes and skirt off to take a bath, she said, "Oh, you need to lose some weight," I asked her, "Why did you say that?" She stated, "Because you have gained weight." Then I reminded her of the time when I first lost weight, I was really small she told me I was too small I needed to gain weight. For her to tell me now I need to lose weight was very hurtful, because I was confused on what made her say this to me. I'm not overweight at all, so to hear her say that and not have a true concern about my well-being as a person hurt me to the core. Lord I need to get off this cycle. I felt that I wasn't good enough; as if yet again I didn't measure up to my mother's standards only to find out I may never measure up to her standards if I was trying to. As a human, her standards are ever changing, but you, oh God, are the only one who is still the same yesterday, today and forever. You are unchangeable and if I behold you as my standards that I should measure to, it will be the same. You are in control of my life and you accept me. I can rest in You and I measure up to Your standards, not man.

I realize how my lack of honor for my parents' lead me to a self-destructive life as evidenced by what I have disclosed thus far. In the book, *Cleansing The Sanctuary of The Heart: Tool for Emotional Healing*, David and Beverly answers the question of what it means to honor our parents even though they may have done some very hurtful things to us. *"The answer is, the law, God's law, requires us to honor them, because of their position in our life. Honor does not mean we agrees with what they have or haven't done, but we treat them with due obedience and courtesy because of their position as mother or father."* Your manager is your manager and you get to disagree with how he or she does things, but the role must be honored.

I have been on this healing of the heart, mindset transformation and relationship reconciliation journey for four years, and in 2016 I can truly say I honor my parents. Through much prayer, counseling, coaching, journaling and sobbing, I have gotten to a place of acceptance with my parents and I'm able to honor them now for who they are. It hasn't been an easy journey. There has been a lot of back and forth, blaming, shaming, being a victim, being dismissive or taking flight in the conversation and relationship, but through all the pain we have come out on the other side and life is a little bit clearer.

BIBLICAL SPOTTING

(Luke 13:6-9) tells the story of a vineyard owner, a vinedresser, and a fig tree. In this story, the vineyard owner is God, the Vinedresser is Jesus, and the vineyard is the earth, the fig tree is humanity, or you and me. The vineyard owner comes to his vineyard looking for fruit on his fig tree. The fruit that He looked for was a reflection of His character, which is the fruit of the Spirit according to (Galatians 5: 22-23 AMP), *"But the fruit of the [Holy] Spirit [the work which His presence within accomplishes] is love, joy (gladness), peace, patience (an even temper, forbearance), kindness, goodness (benevolence), faithfulness, Gentleness (meekness, humility), self-control (self-restraint, continence)."*

Unfortunately the Vineyard owner didn't find any fruit on the fig tree. The Vineyard owner, God, was ready to release the fig tree as he stated for three years I looked for fruit on this same tree and I haven't found none. He instructed the Vinedresser, Jesus, to cut the tree down, because it was taking up space ".....He said to the vinedresser, why should it continue also to use up the ground [to deplete the soil, intercept the sun, and take up room]" taking all it can from all sources without giving back to the earth. The vinedresser, Christ, replied to the vineyard owner, God, "Leave it alone Sir for one more year, allow me to work with it, he or she, to dig around the roots and put manure on the soil." Manure is excrement from an animal. Manure comes from a source apart from the unfruitful tree that stinks and smells. Jesus was saying allow me to dig around the roots, and use someone else's mess to awaken the person. The roots is the source of the problem, the lack of fruit on a tree although it doesn't display signs of decay to the eye, has an issue at the roots, and the root issue will play out on the surface by not producing fruit, (Luke 13:7-8 AMP).

Roots are one of the most vital parts of a tree. They are responsible for receiving nutrients, water intake, store energy, and anchor the tree. Jesus knowing this wants to dig around the roots and put manure on them. In order to put the manure (mess) on the roots, they first have to be exposed to direct light, through the digging process. Though this process can be painful, if the vinedresser it's careful in the digging around the roots, he could hit several roots and over expose the tree to other hazardous things that could harm the tree. Therefore the vinedresser is very careful when digging around the roots to not overly expose the tree. I'm grateful that the vinedresser is Christ and He knows just how much we can bear even when we don't know.

We are likened to the tree that's referred to in the parable. God comes looking for His character in us, and when it's not seen the process to begin. The Spirit is our Vinedresser. The roots of our life are the dark places that we try to keep hidden. The Spirit of God comes to us to reveal and expose the hidden places of our life so we may bear the fruit of God's character. Relationship with people serves as our fertilizer and through our interaction and in relationship the process unfolds.

SPOTTING PROCESS

- **God spots us** He's not able to see His character in us. (Luke 13:6) the certain man came looking for fruit on the fig tree, also (Genesis 3:9)

    (2 Samuel 11 and 12), David and Bathsheba story, God saw how David was moving around.

God came looking for fruit in me, and it couldn't be found.

- **Conversation and Plan** Christ, who sees us deeper than our surface and also minister to or be manure for us comes to us through humanity. (Luke 13:8), Jesus replied, "Leave it alone, the fig tree, for a year and allow me to work with, he or she, to see what happens. (2 Samuel 12:1-4 AMP) AND THE Lord sent Nathan to David. He came and said to him, *"There were two men in a city, one rich and the other poor. The rich man had very many flocks and herds, but the poor man had nothing but one little ewe lamb which he had bought and brought up, and it grew up with him and his children. It ate of his own morsel, drank from his own cup, lay in his bosom, and was like a daughter to him. Now a traveler came to the rich man, and to avoid taking one of his own flock or herd to prepare for the wayfaring man who had come to him, he took the poor man's lamb and prepared it for his guest."*

Christ sent the Into His Rest Ministries team into my life.

- **Judging or Blaming**- The person responds by judging or blaming the situation or story. They have spotted themselves although it's not clear to them.

(2 Samuel 12:5-6) *"Then David's anger was greatly kindled against the man, and he said to Nathan, As the Lord lives, the man who has done this is a son [worthy] of death. He shall restore the lamb fourfold, because he did this thing and had no pity."* At my third retreat there was a woman there who I saw so clearly and I had so much to say about her story. I judged her story only to find out I was her and I didn't like what I saw, which was myself.

- **Revelation**- It's revealed that what we spotted was actually our issue as well.

(2 Samuel 12:7 AMP) *"Then Nathan said to David, You are the man! Thus says the Lord, the God of Israel: I anointed you king of Israel, and I delivered you out of the hand of Saul."*

Before the end of the retreat, God whispered in my ear that I was the lady who I could see so clearly.

- **Consequences-** Although God is merciful we still have consequences for our actions and we have to deal with them with grace.

(2 Samuel 8-12), *"And I gave you your master's house, and your master's wives into your bosom, and gave you the house of Israel and of Judah; and if that had been too little, I would have added that much again. Why have you despised the commandment of the Lord, doing evil in His sight? You*

have slain Uriah the Hittite with the sword and have taken his wife to be your wife. You have murdered him with the sword of the Ammonites.

Now, therefore, the sword shall never depart from your house, because [you have not only despised My command, but] you have despised Me and have taken the wife of Uriah the Hittite to be your wife. Thus says the Lord, Behold, I will raise up evil against you out of your own house; and I will take your wives before your eyes and give them to your neighbor, and he shall lie with your wives in the sight of this sun. For you did it secretly, but I will do this thing before all Israel and before the sun."[Fulfilled in II Sam. 16:21, 22.]AMP God was merciful to me regarding consequences of purging. I had only two teeth decay instead of all of them from the purging.

- **Acknowledgement**- We then look at what we did and acknowledge we have sinned against God. (2 Samuel 12:13 AMP), And David said to Nathan, *"I have sinned against the Lord."*

- **Grace**- Grace is extended to us, we don't get what the law requires.

    (2 Samuel 12:13-14) AMP, And, Nathan said to David, *"The Lord also has put away your sin; you shall not die. (Psalms 51.) Nevertheless, because by this deed you have utterly scorned the Lord and given great occasion to the*

enemies of the Lord to blaspheme, the child that is born to you shall surely die." David life was spared although what was produced through the sin died.

- **Bargaining-** We seek God for a change of heart because we don't like the consequences.

  (2 Samuel 12:16-17), AMP *"David therefore besought God for the child; and David fasted and went in and lay all night [repeatedly] on the floor. His older house servants arose [in the night] and went to him to raise him up from the floor, but he would not, nor did he eat food with them."*

  Before closing the business, I pleaded with God to do something different after I realized that closing was a part of my consequences as it was a byproduct of sinful behavior.

- **Repentance**- We see how we have sinned against God and repent, have a godly sorrow because we realize our action affected more than ourselves.

  (Psalms 51), I believe David wrote this during his bargaining with God, but through the process he repented for his sin.

- **Acceptance**- We see how we sinned against God and we accept the consequences that God hath set before us are just, merciful and full of grace.

(2 Samuel 12: 20-23), AMP *"Then David arose from the floor, washed, anointed himself, changed his apparel, and went into the house of the Lord and worshiped. Then he came to his own house, and when he asked, they set food before him, and he ate. Then his servants said to him, What is this that you have done? You fasted and wept while the child was alive, but when the child was dead, you arose and ate food. David said, While the child was still alive, I fasted and wept; for I said, Who knows whether the Lord will be gracious to me and let the child live? But now he is dead; why should I fast? Can I bring him back again? I shall go to him, but he will not return to me."*

- **Seeing God**- When we accept what is, and be accountable for our actions, we see God through the process. (2 Samuel 12:24-25), AMP, *"David comforted Bathsheba his wife, and went to her and lay with her; and she bore a son, and she called his name Solomon. And the Lord loved [the child]; He sent [a message] by the hand of Nathan the prophet, and [Nathan] called the boy's [special] name Jedidiah [beloved of the Lord], because the Lord [loved the child]. The person that Christ uses in the earth to be the manure will later have favor in our sight according to Proverbs 28:23 AMP, "He who rebukes a man shall afterward find more favor than he who flatters with the tongue."*

This process started with God seeing us looking for His reflection and couldn't find it. He's willing to go to any length for us. He allowed His Son to step into our story to make an impact, and boy am I glad Christ was and still is willing to intervene. The power of relationship, community and storytelling is sown through this process. Christ sent someone to David that he respected and or was in relationship with him already, to share a story with him; through the story he was able to reflect what he saw.

The process ends with us seeing God and beholding Him, which He desires. Once we see God we can behold Him and look to Him to fill us up when we are void and missing unmet love need.

SPOTTING YOURSELF IN SOMEONE ELSE'S STORY

Fast forward to the 21st century. What does it look like to spot oneself in someone else's story as they share it? While on a call with my family; dad, mother, sister, and I, my sister shared with my mother her truth at that moment. She told my mom that she felt unimportant and unworthy of her time. "When I asked you to come to my house and you can't or you don't have time, even though I live, no more than, five minutes from you, I feel unimportant. I want to spend more time with you, but it's as if you are always busy or have something else to do." After she shared, my dad spoke and stated he understood what my sister was saying, "I feel the same way about you all, Jamella & Sherita, I feel unimportant and unworthy because I want to hang out and spend time with you all, but you all are always so busy." He spotted himself in my sister's story. I never knew my dad felt like this and we may not have ever known if my sister hadn't shared her story. Because of her sharing we were all blessed, we all had the same feeling towards one another and in the midst of her telling her story we spotted ourselves.

The manure that the vinedresser referred to as fertilizer can equate to someone else's story that may be painful, devastating, or chaotic. The manure speaks to the root issue of the hearer, which allows them to spot themselves and the reason they are not bearing fruit. I've learned on this journey that storytelling is what we are called to do. I share my story when guided by the Spirit because in my manure someone will find hope. *"And they have overcome (conquered) him by means of the blood of the Lamb and by the utterance of their testimony, for they did not love, and cling to life even when forced with death [holding their lives cheap till they had to die for witnessing]."* (Rev. 12:11 AMP)

As I wrote this chapter, I sipped a cup of Yogi Tea. Each bag has a quote attached and the quote on this bag was befitting for this chapter, *"Recognize that the other person is you."* These are words to live by when we find ourselves blaming, judging or criticizing others.

Truly Shine

Your future may seem to be grimy and dark, because you're at this place at this moment in time.

You're at a blessed place, because there's one direction from here, and it's up, out the grime and mire!

How long you stay here is all up to you, you must do the work, which will cause you to move.

Move to the next place in your life and in time, where the Light within you cannot be dimmed but shine.

There's a journey to get to where you desire to be, just stay focused and encouraged and you will be set free.

Know that you are not alone on the journey, wherever you are, there are others along these roads some near and some far.

When you feel discouraged and want to throw the towel in, reach outside of yourself for support to be empowered by others who have been in the position you're in.
You can and will make it through and your Light will shine, and others will know that someone greater is with you.

Embrace this place in your life and in time. Pay attention to the process and what it takes for your Light to truly shine!

Chapter 7
Resilient Soul

"So, have no fear of them; for nothing is concealed that will not be revealed, or kept secret that will not become known."
(Matthew 10:26), AMP

My journey to wholeness began with a willingness to be exposed. One of my favorite quotes, that I say, states, *"In time all things will be revealed, there is no hidden thing that won't be uncovered and no secret thing that won't be revealed."*

THE EXPOSURE

I can remember in 2013, when I began to speak, God gave me this message titled, "Respect the Process of Deliverance," the story was taken from (John 11), the story of Lazarus death and Resurrection. In this story, Lazarus' sisters, Mary and Martha sent a word to Jesus that Lazarus was dying. Jesus was in another town, about two miles away, and didn't come immediately after receiving the heartbreaking message; his friend was about to die. He waited two days to journey to the town where Lazarus laid. Upon arriving he was greeted by Martha who was upset with his late arrival and disbelief had filled her spirit. Then Mary came to Jesus, she was filled with sadness and faith as she fell to his feet and sobbed. When Christ notices her sobbing and all those who came with her, he was deeply moved and troubled in His Spirit and He wept. He was moved with compassion and proceeded to the grave to make Lazarus and those watching whole. He was met with disbelief as he instructed the people to remove the stone, but He still moved with purpose to set the captives free.

In verse 42, Jesus being at the tomb called Lazarus forth by saying with a loud voice, *"Lazarus come forth."* I can imagine the call to Lazarus was with authority and power. I heard a pastor say there may have been another Lazarus in the grave that day, but they didn't come forth because the call wasn't for their wholeness it was for a specific person. Although others may have the same name as you or me, when God makes a call for wholeness, it's personal. Jesus then said to the grave cloth that had him bound, "Loose him and let him go." Now my imagination takes me somewhere with this story. Jesus allowed Lazarus life story to get as far gone as we in our humanity can see. Lazarus was dead an all could see, it doesn't get any more exposed than that. Everyone knew and saw him. Lazarus was the only person unaware of his own death according to (Ecclesiastes 9:5). He was dead and his sister, Martha, had no faith for him in verse 39 she mentioned to Jesus that he was decaying and putting off an offensive odor. I'm sure his state of existence or non-existence appeared hopeless to her and others watching. Jesus demonstrated that no matter how far gone one may appear to be, we are never beyond his capacity to save. Jesus's call went to the depth of his soul, Lazarus came forth, exposed and still bound in grave cloth.

When Jesus calls us forth, we are still bound and our process of deliverance and wholeness began. We all have a process to go through before we can walk out our freedom in Christ. During Biblical times, the bodies were wrapped with linens. I'm thinking they looked like the mummified bodies shown in history books or in movies. I imagined this is how Lazarus was bound. The bodies would be wrapped with white linen from the feet to the head, binding the body where it's confined within its bounds. Imagine Lazarus coming forth bound, I see him hopping because his feet, although loosened, were still bound or he walked really slowly towards the entrance of the tomb. The body was wrapped from bottom up, but I believe it was released from the grave cloth from top down. I believe it was released from top down because Lazarus was being transformed from one state to another and we are instructed according to (Romans 12:2)… "be ye transformed by the renewing of your mind."

DELIVERANCE PROCESS

- **Mindset shift**- His thought processes, perception, and understanding of who Jesus was changed by his experience with Jesus. Before his death he only had mere knowledge of Jesus. Knowledge without experience is not enough for the transformation that we must go through. Lazarus now had an experience. Ephesians reads, *"That you may really come, to know, practically, through experience for yourselves, the love of Christ, which far surpasses mere knowledge, without experience; that you may be filled, through all your being, unto all the fullness of God, may have the richest measure of the divine Presence, and become a body wholly filled and flooded with God Himself!"* (Ephesians 3:19, AMP)

  Imagine he's being unwrapped from the grave cloth and the crown of his head is unwrapped therefore his mindset, perception, and understanding is being shifted.

- **Eyes open to see**- Our experience determines how we view or see a situation. If our life experience has been perceived as negative, then that's how we do life, with the lenses of negatively. Once Lazarus's mindset shifted, his eyesight was different. The eye is the lamp of the body. So if your eye is sound, your entire body will be full of light. (Matthew 6:22 AMP)

Continue to imagine the grave cloth being unwrapped!

- **Ears of understanding**- When we experience Christ we hear differently, understanding comes through hearing. *"Incline your ear [submit and consent to the divine will] and come to Me; hear, and your soul will revive; and I will make an everlasting covenant or league with you, even the sure mercy (kindness, goodwill, and compassion) promised to David."* (Isaiah 55:3 AMP). We are still unwrapping the grave cloth, so what's next?

And his ears were opened, his tongue was loosed, and he began to speak distinctly and as he should. (Mark 7:35 AMP)

- **Nose to breathe and mouth to speak-** His nose and mouth were loosed. He could now breathe clearly and speak of the things his ears heard, eyes seen and his transformed mind comprehended. *"O Lord, open my lips, and my mouth shall show forth Your praise."* (Psalm 51:15 AMP)

The grave cloth would continue to unravel and more of his body would be loosed, his neck, shoulders, upper arms his chest area which houses vital organs.

- **Beating Heart** - Through Lazarus' experience with Jesus, his heart could beat with compassion for those that he can now see are still bound, because he's acquainted with their sufferings. His head and heart will line up and he will live with balance. Lazarus through his experience, "Become useful and helpful and kind to one another, tenderhearted (compassionate, understanding, loving-hearted), forgiving one another [readily and freely], as God in Christ forgave you." (Ephesians 4:32 AMP).

Continue to imagine the grave cloth being unwrapped from his body. The top portion of his body has unwrapped and he is almost fully exposed.

- **Touch of compassion**- His hands are now free he can expend his hand for help when he needs it and can also be help when someone else in need. *"Instantly Jesus reached out His hand and caught and held him, saying to him, O you of little faith, why did you doubt?"* (Matthew 14:31 AMP).

The grave cloth continued to unravel and now his thighs are free and he's able to move just a little. The wrapping is falling down, his lower legs are free and he can move much better while he stands naked and exposed in the tomb. When Jesus called him forth from the dead state and he saw himself exposed, I imagine fear of what people thought began to settle in. Even though the miracle was more about Christ and his power, Lazarus was simply a tool or vessel that was available for Christ's glory.

- **Move freely**- His feet are released and he can now move freely and go as Christ would send him. *"And having shod your feet in preparation [to face the enemy with the firm-footed stability, the promptness, and the readiness produced by the good news] of the Gospel of peace."* (Ephesians 6:15, AMP)

I was Lazarus. Imagine if you could with me that you are Lazarus. As you read, reflect on what deadness you are being called out of. Imagine Jesus saying your name and telling you to come forth. Where are you in your process? Are you just hearing his voice? Has your grave cloth began to unravel and you have knowledge, but compassion and experience is elusive? Are you extending your hand for help? Are you standing at the entrance of the tomb exposed and needing Jesus to extend his hand to walk you into the light? Are you standing and or walking in the light naked and exposed, with Christ rode over your nakedness. We are all at different places in our journey, but we are headed in the same direction, wholeheartedness. Lazarus was healed when he was called forth, but wholeness was activated through the removal of the grave cloth.

My journey and cloth unraveling began in 2009. I heard the Holy Spirit say, "Jamella, come forth." Not only was I bound by bulimia, but I was being held hostage. The bulimia was connected to the molestation, rejection, dysfunctional family, self- defeating thoughts, self-hatred, and shame was at my core. Through all that stuff, I still heard the voice of Christ with authority through one of his servants, Pastor Willie Black.

Pastor Black said, "Jamella Stroud come forth," by way of being the church clerk. I was hesitant in my response, but once I said, yes, my life has not been the same. I accepted a position in my childhood church as the clerk in 2009 and functioned in that position in 2010. Although I faced opposition I was still determined to come forth. The process of deliverance is indeed a process and coming from a spiritual deadness isn't instant, it's work, internal work. Paul described this work in (Hebrews 4:11) KJV, *"Let us labour therefore to enter into that rest, lest any man fall after the same example of unbelief."* Our labor, is to do the heart work to move from deadness to rest; internal rest, peace, awareness, joy, meekness, and gentleness. We can only enter this rest once we come forth and the grave cloth unravel.

When I became the clerk not everyone was excited. I experienced opposition from those around me. Everyone is not going to agree with our freedom and being called forth. Most of the pushback is from those closest to us, it hurts and is very painful to hear, experience, and witness their reaction to your process. There were those who question my ability to operate in the position. I had to go before them to explain why I was qualified for the position. Although I was a college graduate with a Bachelor's degree in social and behavioral science and an Associate of Science in office administration, I also had the business at the time; I still had to prove I was qualified. More importantly, if I didn't have any of that, the fact that God called me forth and all that I didn't have that I would need he would equip me in the process. That was a painful time, what I learned from the experience was, "I'm not enough, which was shame's language. Who do she think she is? Isn't she Jimmy and Gaynell's daughter?"

Nevertheless, Christ called me forth and I moved in spite of the opposition, despite the fact that I was molested, bulimic, and had liposuction on my thighs, I was on Section 8 and food stamps, I was a single mother, my child's father was deceased, I was in a relationship and participating in premarital sex and full of shame. I was called forth like Lazarus and began to hop towards the entrance of my tomb bound in all the grave cloth, but yet still moving towards Jesus, who represented healing and wholeness. Like any tomb it was dark, but I could see the light as I moved closer towards the entrance.

In 2011, I began to really study the Bible for myself and started my spiritual journey. I was renewing my mind and my grave clothes were coming off. In July of 2011, I went on a mission trip to St. Lucia with my church. I went on the trip with impure motives, but I received so much more. God took me across the waters to sit me down so He could talk with me and get me out of my comfort zone. There wasn't anything required of me on this trip, no building, working, or speaking, nothing. I was sent on this trip by God to be, not to do. Being didn't come easy because I lived my life in performance mode trying to find the next thing to do. I began to hear God speak to me. I dedicated my body back to Christ and I vowed for celibacy until marriage. I learned the joy of simplicity. The trip was three weeks, but I only stayed two weeks because while I was away everything at home and in the businesses seemed to be falling apart and I left prematurely.

Unbeknownst to me, God was doing something within me during that time to see what could cause me to not continue to follow Him. My daughter was back in the states with my family, well with my dad. She was hurt in a bike accident, the business flooded; things appeared to be going crazy while I was away for those two weeks. I didn't really understand the stumbling block would be thrown in my path during the process. As stated, I came home prematurely to handle those things, although I had to pay more money to change my plane ticket. My experience those two weeks were internally transformational.

I continued to read and study for myself and I began to see spiritual things. I first began to see others more clearly, although Christ wanted me to see myself first. This came a little later in my process, my ability to see myself. My ears were unwrapped and I could hear what the Divine Spirit was saying to me. Through my daughter I heard God speak, not that she said thus saith the Lord, but I began to pay attention to her and I received messages from God through her, about myself.

In 2013, my mouth was unwrapped and I began to speak at my church, other churches, and all throughout the community. There was opposition all around me during this time. I met a guy at church who was a new member, and I thought he was sent by God to be my husband, but he wasn't. After dating him a few months, I discovered he was a reflection of my dad. If you remember my dad from earlier chapters he was his mirror image. When I say he was my dad's mirror, I mean some of the same struggles my dad had, he had. He was addicted to crack cocaine and emotional unavailable just like my dad. I allowed him to live in my home not once, but three different times for a few months at a time. I did this all in the name of helping him, I related to him the same way I related to my dad as a little girl, and I became his caretaker. I was truly in denial about where I was and the internal pain that lived deep within.

Although this was a non-sexual relationship it was still devastating to see the pain I carried and inflicted on my daughter and him through this relationship. He was sent to reveal to me my pain that I still carried regarding my dad. I was still on my journey to wholeness during this time and speaking at churches and within the community. I was addicted to the addict in him, which was a reflection of my dad and the parts of my dad that I judged or made internal vows about. I handled my relationship with him how I handled my dad's, and it was unhealthy. All the things I hadn't accepted, judged or made a vow about concerning my dad, I experienced through him. In my eyes, my dad was weak because he was on drugs, dismissive, and minimized everything. I treated this guy as if he was helpless when the reality was; I was codependent and functioned in his dysfunction.

A few weeks ago while writing this book, I had the opportunity to spend some time with my dad and his mother. I realized from my interactions with them why my dad is the way he is. He's a byproduct of his family, as we all are at some point in life. As a child, I hadn't known that my grandmother was really bitter and hurt because she grew up without her parents, and she was a victim all the time. I listened to her and in her story someone was always doing things to her, life was never positive. I made unconscious internal vows and judgments about my dad, and the Bible is true, when we are told to judge not, lest we be judged according to (Matthew 7:1) AMP, therefore I lived out those vows and judgments, but God is mighty to save.

I met the Sedlacek's during the time I was entangled in the dysfunctional relationship, in Alabama, as they facilitated a seminar. I heard them present and share their story and I knew that they were who I needed to connect with at this part of the journey.

I purchased their book *Cleansing the Sanctuary of the Heart*, and again I had impure motivations or shall I say I was in denial about my true heart condition. Because I purchased the book with the mind that I would read it to help other young girls, but the little girl within me, was in need of help and healing. I contacted Beverly Sedlacek later on and she informed me of an emotional healing retreat that JoAnne Palmer and Andrea Blackburn facilitated. She invited me to attend and I was excited. I was supposed to attend my first retreat in October of 2013, but I didn't go. I continued to read their book and I began to see myself and my heart issues just a bit clearer.

In 2014, I continued to read the book to learn more about my heart condition being that it was the next thing to be released. In April of the same year, my mother and I went to our first retreat where I encountered and experienced Christ through some of the ways I read about. After the retreat, I joined their weekly conference calls. Later in 2014 I attended another retreat and was accompanied by my mother, sister, grandmother, and friend. I was determined to be free, my heart issues were made more clearer as my grave clothes were being unraveled and my vital organs were being released, I could began to breathe because I was able to truly see my heart. According to (Jeremiah 17:9) AMP *"The heart is deceitful above all things, and it is exceedingly perverse and corrupt and severely, mortally sick! Who can know it [perceive, understand, be acquainted with his own heart and mind,"* my heart was deceitful to me. I believed God wanted me to be in an unhealthy relationship and he wanted me to put my daughter and myself in harm's way. In my mind, He wanted me to be a martyr, to try to "save" someone else, when in reality I needed help myself first to see my true heart condition before I could see someone else's heart condition. The God that I knew from my experience was harsh and He was waiting for me to make the next wrong move so He could punish me. I learned about this God through my initial understanding of God through my family of origin, my mother was the disciplinarian and that was the God she knew through her experience. As children of God, our first experience of Him is through our parents or caregivers, according to the Sedlacek's.

NAKEDNESS

"Come now, and let us reason together, says the Lord. Though your sins are like scarlet, they shall be as white as snow; though they are red like crimson, they shall be like wool." (Isaiah 1:18 AMP) My head, heart, and torso area was now uncovered. I imagined Lazarus standing in the tomb about to step into the light now naked and exposed because his grave cloth began to fall off. I reflect back to (Genesis 3:7) AMP, *"Then the eyes of them both were opened, and they knew that they were naked; and they sewed fig leaves together and made themselves apron like girdles..."* Shame fell upon them when they saw themselves. The reality is they were already naked, God saw them just as they were, but they didn't see themselves. Once the eyes of my heart were opened, shame consumed me. I wanted to run back into my tomb and wrap myself up with my

grave clothes. When I realized I was no different from the guy I dated, I was a victim, who due to my brokenness, became a victimizer and it was demonstrated through that relationship. When I saw that all the shame and blame I felt from my mother as a child, because of the vows and judgments I did the same thing to others and my child, I was devastated. I realized I was like my dad I lived in denial for quite some time and I was deceitful and manipulative, too. I saw myself as a controlling boss whose work environment was full of shame, leaving my employees with a feeling that they were not good enough, I wanted to run and cover myself with my grave clothes all over again once I saw these things, but that was no longer an option anymore because Christ had called me forth. I choose to own it, all of it not hiding anything anymore and use it for God's glory.

On the journey to wholeness, standing naked is pivotal, being able to be seen by humanity unashamed or shall I say have intimacy or Into Me See, with humanity. We are told, *"Come now, and let us reason together, says the Lord. Though your sins are like scarlet, they shall be as white as snow; though they are red like crimson, they shall be like wool."* (Isaiah 1:18 AMP) We don't have to try to cover ourselves we must expose ourselves and allow Christ to cover us.

While on a family trip to Dallas, Texas my uncle, my dad's brother, took us to Spa Castle. This spa was unique in many ways. Upon arriving, we parked outside this huge edifice that indeed looked like a castle. My uncle, grandmother, sister, and myself, walked into the facility and purchased our admission into the spa. The men and women were separated; therefore my grandmother, sister and myself went to the women's side on the right, while my uncle went to the left, men's side. Once we entered the locker room area two Asian female employees greeted us. They asked our clothing size and handed us pink and gray pants and shirt and instructed us to put our current clothing into a designated locker. Before we could put their clothes on we were instructed to go to the bathing spa area to shower and or sit in the one of the bathing spas.

To enter the bathing lounge we had to be naked, yes I said naked or shall I say, nude. We were not in isolation naked we had to be naked in front of all the other women there in the bathing lounge. Everyone was naked; there were no formal towels only hand towels, that weren't big enough to cover the entire body. When we discovered that we had to be naked I said to my sister here we go, "When in Rome do as the Romans do," so I unclothed myself and headed to the bathing spa lounge unashamedly with the other women, who were also unclothed. Everyone there was also "naked" and unashamed, we were all in the same situation although we were from different walks of life, cultures, nationality, socio-economic status and class. Even if I felt shame and reached for a towel they weren't big enough to cover the length of our bodies.

My sister wasn't comfortable with this idea so she in her best efforts attempted to cover herself by placing three of the hand towels over herself, but her best efforts didn't fully cover her nakedness, it revealed her attempt to hide. Through her efforts, she tried to hide and became the odd person in the environment because everyone else was free to be even though their nakedness was exposed.

WHY NAKEDNESS AND EXPOSURE

According to Spa Castle's website, tx.spacastleusa.com, "Since the beginning of bathing history clothing was prohibited inside the tubs for sanitary reasons. Unnatural chemicals and toxins from the clothing would be drawn out by the intense heat of the water and absorbed into the pores and skin. It was also said that a bather wearing clothing in this area was trying to conceal an unhealthy condition that was, in his or her mind, worth hiding. To promote the cleanest water for the bathers and stay true to ancient bath traditions, clothing and or any form of bathing suits are prohibited inside all locker room baths."

In the Book of Genesis, we see where clothing was prohibited in the Garden of Eden. Man and woman walked freely before God in their nakedness. It wasn't until after sin entered the heart of man and woman that they attempted to cover themselves as described in (Genesis 3:7). Clothing was or shall I say hiding was, is unnatural. The reality is they were always naked, but it wasn't until they saw themselves that they tried to cover themselves. Clothing, like in ancient times with bathers, meant a person is trying to conceal or hide something that he or she deemed as unhealthy as stated earlier. Sin and the shame associated with it has caused us to hide and be unaware of our hiding. To see ourselves naked and exposed, which is our own heart condition initially can cause us to hide behind a shame core, control/controlling, self-reliance and other things that on the list in Chapter 5.

The Bible doesn't record this, but I imagine Jesus saying to Lazarus, "Its okay. Lazarus, come on out, I'm right here." Lazarus stood paralyzed by fear at the entrance of the tomb. I can even imagine Jesus going to meet Lazarus in the tomb, even though he was being exposed; Jesus got really close and covered him with His robe of righteousness. Although he was naked, he saw Jesus' face first, which allowed him to despise the shame of his own nakedness because his eyes were now focused on the one who called him forth and covered him. Therefore staying in the tomb and hiding trying to piece the grave cloth together wasn't favorable to him and he continued to come forth.

I totally get and understand hiding and standing naked and afraid in a tomb of which I had been released. The first poem in this book "Caged Bird" tells that story. On this journey, everything seemed to be falling off, all the covering, control, self- reliance, performing, addiction, and being a victim. I tried to hide due to shame. Over the course of 24 months my nakedness was being exposed. I closed the business's two locations. I moved away from my family. My daughter got into her first fight at a church event and I had to drive three hours to get her, because she was dismissed. I had no money due to purging financially. I was depressed. My rent was one month late and I received an eviction notice, went to court and was ordered to move, but God intervened. I had issues with my daughter getting into trouble at school. I, after getting a financial counselor and coming up with a budget to pay off debt, still filed bankruptcy. All this was going on in my life and hiding or staying in my tomb appeared to be easy, but God still spoke come forth. Now I stand naked!

Naked

Naked

Open, exposed, all can see!

See! What you're made to be.

Be, who God has created you, you are so beautiful.
Beautiful isn't a characteristic; it's who you are! You're naked!
Not hiding behind anything.
Being exposed to Him, who created all things! You're free!
Out of all the boxes that man created you to be in.

With me you're Free, Naked, Open, Exposed!

For salvation and the healing of the nations we all have to stand naked before humanity exposing the unhealthy parts as with ancient bathing, to promote clean waters and be a wellspring of life for those who thirst for righteousness again for the healing of the nations and the wholeness of our souls.

WALKING OUT

Lazarus' feet is now released, and he has walked or hopped and made his way to the entrance of the tomb, his transformation had begun, renewing of his mind, his eyes are open, ears can hear, mouth speaks, heart understands hands extended with compassion exposed and naked, but covered with Christ robe of righteousness. He stands in the light and Christ said to them, "Loose him, and let him go," according to (John 11:44 KJV). The Bible doesn't say who Jesus was talking to when He said this. Was He speaking to the people watching? Was it angels who know were present, or was it forces of darkness? I believe Jesus spoke to the forces of darkness that bound him in the first place. Death was conquered, but it comrades shame and its companions fear, distrust, and anxiety were still presence. Christ spoke with such authority even these toxic bounds couldn't hold Lazarus and he was totally free as he abided in Christ.

The Scripture doesn't record this, but I believe once he was released completely, he went with his sisters and ate. I can imagine him starving spiritually and physically and many people followed him and his sisters. I can see the people being inquisitive about what he had experienced because his story preceded him and was the foundation of his ministry. That's my story about Lazarus story, but Lazarus's story is also my story. Although I wasn't physically dead bulimia was death, all the behavior produced death instead of life.

I had a dental appointment because one of my teeth broke in my mouth, a consequence of bulimia, binging and purging. I had a root canal in the tooth three years ago, but didn't go back to receive the crown. When I went to get the crown, because I didn't have any protection for the tooth it was still susceptible to decay even though the nerve was out of the tooth. The dentist said to me, "Oh my you have so much decay in this tooth and I'm not sure if I can save it." The decay is deep, beyond the gum line, but I'm going to do what I can to save it." I didn't want to have a tooth pulled and have an empty space, but I accepted my reality. I asked God if possible, save it, make it crownable. Well it was crownable, although they had to take some additional steps the dentist had to dig all the decay out, and then place something in my roots for support to make it stronger. They then performed a buildup, which prepared it for the crown.

I am reminded of a promise that say, *"And I am convinced and sure of this very thing, that He Who began a good work in you will continue until the day of Jesus Christ [right up to the time of His return], developing [that good work] and perfecting and bringing it to full completion in you."* (Philippians 1:6 AMP). Although my process began with the root canal three years ago, God is faithful and will finish what he started and it took three years to complete the process and receive the crown. The decay was a reflection of me. I had so much decay in my life and like Martha said in (John 11:39 AMP), *"But Lord by this time he is decaying and throws off an offensive odor......"* Jesus replied, *"Did I not tell you and promise you that if you would believe and rely on me you would see the glory of God."* Christ showed me it doesn't matter how far gone a person appears to be, if he or she is decaying because their life is producing death, there is nothing too hard for Him, if we just believe. Yes, I have to deal with the consequences of binging and purging, but God is sovereign.

Through His providence He dug deep to remove all the decay in my life, place some support in my roots (childhood) by allowing me to see life with a new perspective. He performed a "build up" and sealed me,

(His Spirit), by placing the crown on top of my once decayed tooth or shall I say life. If someone looked into my mouth at first glance he or she wouldn't know I had a root canal and a crown due to the tooth decay, but if they take a closer look they could see the difference. My life is evident as well, although one may not physically see my crown. If you get closer and there is a level of Into Me See (intimacy), you would be able to see that something is different and once I share my story, my Lazarus experience becomes apparent.

Perfectly Imperfect

The place called Perfect oh how I wish it was true, but when I look around and can't find it, I'm left feeling lost and blue.

What does Perfect look like in a human being? Or what does it look like in a material thing? What is the Perfect idea?

We have longed and searched, but our quest has failed.

There's no such thing as Perfect, only imperfect beings and things, But they're all Perfect in the imperfection of things.

There's one Perfect thing that I have found, that's the Love of Christ that has always been around.

Even with His Perfection, I've found there are still ups and even downs.

I allow you to do your Perfect work in me and stand because I am free!
Free to be Perfectly imperfect with you!

Chapter 8
Purpose, Passion & Perspective

Before building a home, one of the first steps in the process is to clear the land by pulling the surface things that are on top of the land down and destroying what was originally there. Then the engineers must excavate the grounds by digging the land to remove things underneath the surface to lay the foundation. The deeper the foundation, the taller the building can stand. Imagine a skyscraper and the outer appearance of it what you don't see is the foundation work and depths of the foundation that's imperative for the massive structure to stand.

The business that God had given me, J'S Tax Service, LLC, had to be demolished, too, the name and the way I did business had to die. It was on the surface and it had to be removed so God could dig deeper to work on a new foundation. As mentioned earlier, I filed bankruptcy and it was a painful, but sobering experience to bankruptcy. There was also beauty in the experience once I understood that bankruptcy was connected to my transformation. I was emotionally bankrupt within; therefore bankruptcy was an outer manifestation of my inward condition. I sat with my truth, I felt, I had nothing to offer. Although I wanted to repay all my debtors, I couldn't, but Christ did.

Through my journey of shutting down, God was using the experience to create passion, purpose, and a new perspective. Before this experience, I was in business with a perverted passion, which was obsessive. My focus was more about the cause to acquire money than it was about serving people. When our passion is perverted, the reason we do what we do has nothing to do with others, but it's about our personal gain. When we cease to get what we wanted we see no value in what we do. Prior to this last year I must confess my passion was indeed perverted and I was obsessed with acquiring money that slipped right through my hand.

This scripture is the embodiment of purpose, "*The Spirit of the Lord is upon Me*," perspective, Christ was able to see and understand clearly; "*because He has anointed Me [the Anointed One, the Messiah] to preach the good news (the Gospel) to the poor; He has sent Me to announce release to the captives and recovery of sight to the blind, to send forth as delivered those who are oppressed [who are downtrodden, bruised, crushed, and broken down by calamity], To proclaim the accepted and acceptable year of the Lord [the day when salvation and the free favors of God profusely abound]*, purpose, Christ spoke his purpose that was given to him by the one who sent him. This is the best elevator pitch I've ever heard. (Luke 4:18-19 AMP). Christ's tone and actions demonstrates his passion for doing what He was sent to do. "*Then He rolled up the book and gave it back to the attendant and sat down; and the eyes of all in the synagogue were gazing [attentively] at Him. And He began to speak to them: "Today this Scripture has been fulfilled in your hearing and in your presence,"* (Luke 4:20-21 AMP), There are some things that took place before He became clear about his purpose, passion and perspective. Earlier in Luke chapter 4, He went through a season of chaos before He got clarity and during that time He had to make some choices that were conducive to him moving close to clarity. According to (Luke 4:1), Jesus was controlled by the Holy Spirit and was led by the Holy Spirit into the wilderness. It wasn't by chance that He went through what He went through it was by design. He had earned something that was going to assist Him on his journey as He moved into His purpose. While in the wilderness for 40 days, He was tempted, tried, and tested by the devil.

The chaos to clarity process:

- **Being without** - He was hungry no food to eat according to (Luke 4:2) for 40 days. After not eating for three days the greatest amount of protein is loss. Protein is where we get energy. Because He was without energy, He became open to receiving from whatever source.

- **Vulnerable** - After being without food which is a necessity for living; He could have submitted to the devil's test when it was suggested several times for

Him, to prove himself as shown in verse three when he was asked to turn the stone into bread. In (Luke 4: 5 -7) He was shown all the things that could belong to him if he would bow down. In (Luke 4: 9-11) when nothing else worked suicide was suggested. Because of Him being without He was vulnerable meaning open to making things happen in His favor to relieve Himself from His current situation. He chose to go through the chaos to gain the clarity.

- **Being defined**- While in His chaos the devil wanted to tell him who he was because his exterior situation didn't appear to be reflective of who he was internally. Although his outside situation didn't line up with what others may think it should look like, he was sure of who he was. With every test he answered with the Word of God. With the first test He said in (Luke 4:4), *"It is written, Man shall not live by bread alone but by every word and expression of God."*

I must note being in the desert, a dry and barren place, wasn't an unknown situation to Jesus because it was somewhere He had been before or grow up according to (Luke 1: 80), And the little boy grew and became strong in spirit; and he was in the deserts (wilderness) until the day of his appearing to Israel [the commencement of his public ministry].

- **Return**- After Christ overcame the test, He went to Galilee and there went out a fame of him, according (Luke 4:14) and He taught in the synagogue. He then went to Nazareth where he had been brought up and went into their synagogue on the Sabbath day and stood up to read according to verse 16.

I am acquainted with Christ's' process of moving from chaos to clarity to have a clear purpose, passion and perspective. On January 2nd, 2015, I moved to Pike Road from Moody, AL for a job at a non-profit organization in which I began working on September 2nd 2014. I moved in distress not knowing what my purpose was in life or business in this dry place. My healing from binging and purging financially was in process. I had recently closed the physical doors on my business, but honestly my heart was still connected to the financial aspect of the business. I didn't want to lose that by moving, but I being led by the Spirit, I moved anyway.

Upon entering this new job, it was exciting for two to three weeks, then the dust settled and I began to see things clearly. I was at this place for change for myself first, then for the organization. I met with the administrative leadership on three occasions about concerns that I had, and all times I walked away feeling some kind of way. Later I found out from a retreat I felt rejected and it was from this place I discovered rejection issues. I needed what happened to happen so I could overcome and look at the root of my rejection. The administration made a statement to me that I didn't understand during the time it was made because it was hurtful. After bringing notice to things that were problematic and providing solution, I was told I could go back to my business if things were not going as I liked because they have always done it that way and that's how things are done. I was crushed because surely I know God led me to this new city and not even a month after moving I was told I can go back to my business. I was totally confused as to what was meant by this statement but the feeling I didn't like. I now felt confused along with rejected.

My Process As It Relates To Christ Story.

Being without - I was sent to this new place, well it wasn't new because, I, like Jesus, had been here before, but I wasn't aware. I came to this town in 2001 for college, but I didn't stay I left prematurely my second semester in school, and became pregnant shortly after leaving. I was without family, friends, support, money, and the ability of choice. The doors appeared to be closing in on me.

Vulnerable - All that I thought I knew about myself and Christ was challenged I resigned from the job in February 2015. I was there for five months exactly. I left because I was without. I felt empty. I was open to be filled like Christ. There were many chances for me to be filled and allow something external to define my being. Christ intervened because although I didn't have external validation I had Christ in me giving me the strength to push through the pain and chaos.

Being Defined - During the summer of 2015, I looked for work, but couldn't find any. I felt helpless, but God continued to provide although I was in the midst of financial bulimia. I thought it was more money that I needed, but in reality God was redefining my faith, trust, and reliance in Him. He was moving me from chaos to clarity that I will live with purpose, passion and a new perspective.

Return - After Jesus was tempted for a season, He being filled with the Holy Spirit, returned to where He grew up and walked in His ministry with purpose, passion and perspective. This book is apart of my assignment here in this place and once it's complete I shall also return to where I grew up and walk in ministry moving from chaos to clarity walking in purpose, passion and perspective.

PURPOSE LEAD

"See, I have this day appointed you to the oversight of the nations and of the kingdoms to root out and pull down, to destroy and to overthrow, to build and to plant." (Jeremiah 1:10 AMP)

The above text is my purpose. While working with a coaching client I was told by her, "When you come around you bring something out of me that I didn't know was there!" On another occasion I was told, "You know you can bring the bad out." I replied, "What!" with a confused look on my face, while thinking that's not good. Then she followed with, "No, I'm not saying in a negative way. You bring the bad out so the good can be revealed and that's a good thing." I exhaled, and accepted her words and the words of (Jeremiah 1:10) mentioned above. My story is about uprooting lies, and negative thought patterns, pulling down structures or walls that keep Christ and humanity out, destroying secrets and generational curses, overthrowing principalities that are enemies of Christ, building communities, faith and trust in Christ and humanity, and planting forgiveness love, hope, peace, patience, gentleness, and understanding.

THE CONCLUSION OF THE MATTER

The road from Bulimic to Believer, chaos to clarity, redefining purpose and passion while gaining a new perspective, has been traveled via the avenue of trust, love and forgiveness! All that is written had to be forgiven and created situations and circumstances for it. I chose to forgive my parents for their role in my life that negatively impacted me. God knew my parents, including myself, would drop the ball somewhere, therefore He already had a plan which is expressed in (Psalms 27:10 NKJV) *"When my father and my mother forsake me, Then the Lord will take care of me."* I chose to forgive myself for the poor choices I made and accepted that I am forgiven as told in (Psalms 103:12 NKJV) *"As far as the east is from the west, So far has He removed our transgressions from us."*

I chose to forgive myself for the judgments and vows I had towards my parents. I forgave myself the negative not believing in myself. I forgave myself for not trusting myself. I forgave myself for the self abuse. I chose to forgive myself for believing my value and worth came from money. I chose to forgive myself for judging myself. I chose to forgive myself for not trusting God. I chose to forgive myself for the pain I inflicted on others. I chose to forgive myself for believing I did not deserve better. I chose to forgive the people who molested me. I chose to forgive those who spoke negatively in my life although sometimes unbeknownst to them. I asked those who were affected by my behavior to forgive me also. Simply put I chose trust, love and forgiveness! "For if you forgive men their trespasses, your heavenly Father will also forgive you. But if you do not forgive men their trespasses, neither will your Father forgive your trespasses." (Matthew 6:14-15 NKJV)

Forgiveness

Oh the journey it had been to release and let go the pain within.

Pain from my past that was never express but suppressed, and escaped through self-violating ways.

Pain that I inflicted on others because my inside was filthy and cluttered.

Oh forgiveness you came and released me from fear, guilt, and shame.

For you are the antidote to the inside pain that tries to go unnoticed.

You are the remedy to letting go and truly being free.

Forgiveness without you, my life would be filled with pain and I would forever be sad, depressed and blue.

But there's a process to getting to you, which is daunting but worthwhile upon reaching you.

Forgiveness as I sit on your hill I look down at the rocky path that I climbed to get to you.

I say it was worth it, because the pain that separated me from you seems so far away and no longer has me enslaved.

I sit on your hill and I can breathe again, two deep breaths in and out. Feeling my breaths is such a delight.

Forgiveness came and rescued me from the suppressed pain that enslaved me.

Enrollment Offer

If you would like to book or work with Jamella Stroud for upcoming seminars, retreats, speaking engagements, coaching or consulting please e-mail: bulimictobeliever@gmail.com include your name, event's name, date, and location of event. Jamella will also travel outside of the United States.

If you would like information about upcoming events, conferences, retreats or speaking engagement visit the website www.jamellastroud.com and sign up for the general list and we will let you know what's going on.

If you would like Jamella Stroud to facilitate Master Mind Master Money seminar or workshop, visit www.abundancemanifesto.guru for detail or email bulimictobeliever@gmail.com

Connect with me on Social Media: Facebook, Twitter, LinkedIn, Instagram, Youtube @Jamellastroud

Also, please feel free to send us your success stories using as you journey and move from Bulimic to Believer. We may publish these in upcoming newsletters or articles.

To learn more about Bulimia Nervosa visit:

https://www.nationaleatingdisorders.org

http://www.helpguide.org/articles/eating-disorders/bulimia-nervosa.htm

References

Chapter 1 Bulimia, A Different Perspective

1. Curt Thompson, M.D, Anatomy of the Soul: Surprising Connection between Neuro- science and Spiritual Practices That Can Transform Your Life and Relationships (Tyndale House Publishers, Inc), 2010

Chapter 4 Emotions Will Make You….

1. Curt Thompson, M.D, Anatomy of the Soul: Surprising Connection between Neuro- science and Spiritual Practices That Can Transform Your Life and Relationships (Tyndale House Publishers, Inc), 2010

Chapter 5 Financial/Business Bulimia

1. David and Beverly Sedlacek, Cleansing the Sanctuary of the Heart: Tools for Emotional Healing (Tate Publishing & Enterprise, LLC), 2008

2. David and Beverly Sedlacek, Cleaning the Sanctuary of the Heart: Tools for Emotional Healing. A Companion Workbook for Personal or Group Use (Restful Heart Publishing), 2011 169

3. Ibid.

4. Curt Thompson, M.D, Anatomy of the Soul: Surprising Connection between Neuro- science and Spiritual Practices That Can Transform Your Life and Relationships (Tyndale House Publishers, Inc), 2010

Chapter 6 You Spot it, You got it

1. David and Beverly Sedlacek, Cleansing the Sanctuary of the Heart: Tools for Emotional Healing (Tate Publishing & Enterprise, LLC), 2008

2. Ibid.

Chapter 7 Resilient Soul Journey To Wholeness

1. David and Beverly Sedlacek, Cleansing the Sanctuary of the Heart: Tools for Emotional Healing (Tate Publishing & Enterprise, LLC), 2008

2. 2016 Spa Castle Inc. (http://tx.spacastleusa.com)